The voice of m

G000091060

Theinspirationalseries™
Overcoming adversity and thriving

Sound Mind
My Bipolar Journey
From Chaos to Composure

BY ERIKA NIELSEN

We are proud to introduce Theinspirationalseries™. Part of the Trigger family of innovative mental health books, Theinspirationalseries™ tells the stories of the people who have battled and beaten mental health issues. For more information visit: www.triggerpublishing.com

THE AUTHOR

Erika Nielsen is a Canadian cellist and writer based in Toronto. Erika has a multi-faceted career as a chamber musician, collaborative artist, orchestral player and educator, spanning Baroque and Classical traditions to contemporary and popular genres. She has performed with artists such as Kanye West and Johnny Reid, and is a graduate of The Glenn Gould School and Queen's University.

Erika is a blog contributor to BPhope.com and is also the author of the mental health blog soundmindbook.com. A passionate educator, Erika maintains a busy private studio and is on faculty at National Music Camp of Canada. She is also a visual artist. **celloerika.com**

First published in Great Britain 2018 by Trigger

Trigger is a trading style of Shaw Callaghan Ltd & Shaw Callaghan 23 USA, INC.

The Foundation Centre

Navigation House, 48 Millgate, Newark

Nottinghamshire NG24 4TS UK

www.triggerpublishing.com

Copyright © Erika Nielsen 2018

British Library Cataloguing in Publication Data

A CIP catalogue record for this book is available upon request
from the British Library

ISBN: 978-1-912478-65-1

This book is also available in the following e-Book and Audio formats:

MOBI: 978-1-912478-68-2
EPUB: 978-1-912478-66-8
PDF: 978-1-912478-67-5
AUDIO: 978-1-912478-69-9

Erika Nielsen has asserted her right under the Copyright,
Design and Patents Act 1988 to be identified as the author of this work

Cover design and typeset by Fusion Graphic Design Ltd

Printed and bound in Great Britain by Clays Ltd, Elcograf S.p.A

Paper from responsible sources

www.triggerpublishing.com

Thank you for purchasing this book.
You are making an incredible difference.

Proceeds from all Trigger books go directly to
The Shaw Mind Foundation, a global charity that focuses
entirely on mental health. To find out more about
The Shaw Mind Foundation visit,
www.shawmindfoundation.org

MISSION STATEMENT

Our goal is to make help and support available for every
single person in society, from all walks of life.
We will never stop offering hope. These are our promises.

Trigger and The Shaw Mind Foundation

CONTENTS

A NOTE FROM THE SERIES EDITOR

The Inspirational range from Trigger brings you genuine stories about our authors' experiences with mental health problems.

Some of the stories in our Inspirational range will move you to tears. Some will make you laugh. Some will make you feel angry, or surprised, or uplifted. Hopefully they will all change the way you see mental health problems.

These are stories we can all relate to and engage with. Stories of people experiencing mental health difficulties and finding their own ways to overcome them with dignity, humour, perseverance and spirit.

Erika's story may be familiar with those suffering from a mood disorder. Confused as to why her mood was vacillating all over the place, she put it down to her creativity and love of music. But when, at age 27, she received a diagnosis of bipolar disorder type I, Erika realised that her music could be her lifeline. Through her book, she shares her experiences of living with the disorder both pre- and post-diagnosis, showing how understanding her illness helped her to cope with the disorder, along with the strategies that she implemented to improve her routines. The shock of a new diagnosis and the possible long-term impact is often hard to overcome, but *Sound Mind* proves that it is manageable and, in fact, can be reinterpreted as a positive experience.

This is our Inspirational range. These are our stories. We hope you enjoy them. And most of all, we hope that they will educate and inspire you. That's what this range is all about.

Lauren Callaghan,
Co-founder and Lead Consultant Psychologist at Trigger

Dedicated with love
To my fellow travelers along this road

Trigger Warning: This book contains references to sexual abuse, self-harm, psychosis, and depression.

Disclaimer: Some names and identifying details have been changed to protect the privacy of individuals.

*One must still have chaos within oneself
to give birth to a dancing star.*

Friedrich Nietzsche

PART I

PROLOGUE:
WELCOME TO MY WORLD

music is singing through my head I'm going to be out of ideas for songs I need to express myself I am so sick of the ignorant jerks out there I must express how I feel all the time whether it be through paint or sung by my cello now I'm hungry and I'm in love and I need to paint and dance and swim through my own imagination or else I'll implode or go mad I need more self-discipline or else I'll be a nobody and I think I have potential to be somebody ... somebody who loves everyone and makes the flowers around them blossom cello is so rich and deep like thick chocolate milk and someday I'll cut my hair but not today I feel like I'm dancing and yet I remain still ...

I am 15 years old. I am color and light, music and song. A spinning, sparkling wheel. I am bubbly, charming, creative, passionate, gregarious ... but behind closed doors I am dark, insecure, anxious, tormented, wretched, and worthless. I am mentally ill, but I don't know it.

For 12 more years, I ride this mercurial roller coaster. Up and down. *Way* down ... Then up ... Up ... Screwup. Then down ... Back up ... until I am diagnosed with bipolar disorder: type I, *severe.* I am 27 years old. Who am I now?

*

At the time of my diagnosis, I was a professional cellist and music teacher. I had recently married my darling of eight years, a fellow musician. It was a shock to be diagnosed with a major mental illness just as my life and career was starting to blossom. I was angry and resentful at first, but mostly I was terrified about what it meant for the person I was and who I was about to become.

Was mental illness the source of my creativity? Did *that* account for my kaleidoscopic spirit, my music, and my art? Was bipolar disorder my *real* identity? And what would happen next? Would my cello, with its wordless language—the language that expressed so perfectly who I was and what I longed for—be taken from me? *Please, no.*

Even before I had words, music was integral to my life. Our household and family life were full of music, through good times and bad. As a toddler I listened to my mother teach saxophone, flute, and clarinet, and I sang with my father. I plunked my first songs on the piano long before I started school. I squeaked my violin, and eventually graduated to the cello. I was musically precocious, and at a young age I sensed that music was my vocation and my reason for being. By Grade 8 I knew that I wanted to be a professional musician. A cellist. And though I had doubts and insecurities—as we all do from time to time—music was my reliable companion, my constant. The more we became acquainted, the more I practiced and respected it, and the better our friendship became.

I had a beloved cello teacher while growing up, who identified my innate musicality and encouraged my development. Through hard work I earned an extensive musical education and began a diverse career. Before my diagnosis I had a graduate degree in cello performance from a prestigious institution, ran a full teaching studio, and was the principal cellist of an orchestra. But after? Overnight I became a person with a mental illness. Now I faced a complete life overhaul, and that prospect robbed me of my confidence, identity, and everything I once believed. It left me frightened, isolated, and alone.

I was terrified of "coming out." My work as a freelance musician relied heavily on my reputation, and any slight on artists—from email typos to "difficult" behavior—can be a mark against them. I feared that, despite being a member of a supportive community of artists and musicians—many of whom have "been there"— I would find people hesitant or unwilling to work with me if they knew about my terrible flaw, my bipolar disorder. My *mental illness*.

Despite the fact that 1 in 5 North Americans[1] will experience mental illness at some point in their lifetime, I was still terrified at the reality of being one of them.

I have since learned that it is not only possible to live with a mental health condition, it is possible to live well in every area of life: from your career to your relationships. This includes your day-to-day routines, such as sleep and nutrition. And today—thankfully—art, music, and creativity continue to feature prominently in my life. Though I am still learning, I now feel like I have conquered my bipolar disorder: I live *with* it, not by it or in spite of it. Throughout this bumpy ride I have discovered how to put my mental health first, a discovery that has rippled into creating a life in which I not only function, but thrive.

It is my hope that sharing my firsthand experiences will foster awareness, inspire education, and help erase the stigma surrounding bipolar disorder and other mental health conditions.

Getting to where I am today has required hard work and perseverance. Looking back, I see that I approached understanding my diagnosis with the same thoroughness that I use when learning a new piece of music. I examined my work schedule, stress level, diet, exercise, and sleep cycles. I attended weekly psychiatrist appointments, obtained second and third opinions, underwent intensive psychotherapy, and participated in a weekly bipolar group study. I reached out to bipolar peers, attended support groups, and spent nearly two years finding the right medication combination, all while questioning nearly *three decades* of personal history to make sense of what happened to me. One habit at a time, I was able to reclaim the life and career

I was meant to have. Along the way I discovered what was truly important to me, how I function best, and the power of doing less.

After I was diagnosed, I educated myself by reading detailed manuals, books and articles about bipolar disorder. But what I really wanted was a holistic guide that took a personal approach and addressed the specifics of coping with the illness in day-to-day life. I wanted a guide written by a person who had been there, a person that I could relate to, with ideas on how to move forward and live your best life. I read Kay Redfield Jamison's *An Unquiet Mind* and Ellen Forney's *Marbles*, both of which were wonderful personal stories that described episodes and experiences familiar to me. I found memoirs about rock stars who continued their chaotic, destructive lifestyles and I found manuals written or co-authored by medical practitioners about symptoms and medication. But I never found the relatable story with practical advice that I was looking for.

So I wrote it. In *Sound Mind: My Bipolar Journey From Chaos to Composure*, I share my story as an artist with a common—but not fully accepted—affliction, and I describe the effective holistic health plan and habits that I developed for myself, with the help of my doctors and support team. My success in treating my mental illness through this plan inspired me to pass it along in the hope that it might help others get the right diagnosis, find the support they need, and live the life they were meant to have. I hope this book provides comfort, hope, strength, and inspiration to those living with any mental health issue, from depression and anxiety to bipolar and schizophrenia. I have designed it to be a tool for daily living, with ideas and practical suggestions on how to live well, whatever the diagnosis. My intent is not to outline the medical treatment of bipolar disorder and other mental illnesses, or to explore the details involved in diagnosis beyond my own experience. Much research has been done on bipolar disorder and other mood disorders, with new insights being offered all the time. There are also many great books about the medical specifics of these conditions, which you can explore for yourself.

Sound Mind is divided into two parts. In part I, I share my personal story, the events leading to my bipolar diagnosis, the aftermath, and the steps I took to redesign my life to accommodate my illness. Part II is a guide, where I explain the changes I made in each area of my life. I offer wellness tips and coping strategies that worked for me as I learned to live with bipolar disorder, and I explain how I am able to not only maintain my life and career, but thrive even with my illness. While it is not the same life I lived before my diagnosis, I can proudly say that I have reached a point where life is stable and better than ever.

If you are living with bipolar disorder or another mental health condition, there is now more hope and better treatment available than ever before. As a musician and artist, I am lucky to be part of a community where afflictions of the mind are widely accepted and, sometimes, even expected. That said, even within my community there is a divide between those branded as "true artists"—because their quirky or peculiar behaviors match a romantic notion about creativity—and those who struggle immensely to carry out practical tasks each day.

Creating my blog (soundmindbook.com) and writing for bphope.com (an online magazine for people living with bipolar disorder) felt like a safe way to share my experience. Those who were interested would read, and those who weren't would not. When my blog launched, I was surprised and encouraged to receive an outpouring of support and loving messages from friends and strangers alike. As far as I know, sharing my advice and experiences around my mental health condition has had no negative effect on my work life and reputation. I feel fortunate to be living at a time when there is a positive dialogue about mental illness and mental health and wellness.

That being said, heavy stigma still surrounds people with mental illness, and I have seen it and experienced it firsthand. I was even guilty of it myself, before I really understood! Often this stigma prevents those who are suffering from reaching out, getting the help they need, and accessing available resources. Even after researching bipolar disorder and arming myself with information, I still found it unbelievably difficult and exhausting to explain it to those who didn't yet understand. I have since chosen to go with a "share with those who care" approach, which works well.

Mental health conditions are being talked about more than ever. Now there are elaborate awareness campaigns, conversations both in person and through social media, and discussions about overall wellness, self-care, and work-life balance. While this makes me optimistic, there is still so much work to do.

It has been exactly five years since my diagnosis, and I can't think of a better way to celebrate than sharing *Sound Mind* with you. The opportunity to share one's personal story is a rare privilege and I am honored and humbled that you have taken the time to read mine. I hope you find something in these pages that resonates, heals, or leaves you feeling hopeful. If reading *Sound Mind* helps you take one small step toward your recovery, or fosters an awareness and deeper compassion for those who struggle, I will have achieved my goal in writing this book.

CHAPTER 1

The Language of Music

It's 1980's West Germany. I am settled in front of the TV as *Sesame Street* begins. Big Bird is dressed in a tuxedo, which stands out against his canary-yellow feathers. He introduces a "Honker" and "Dinger" quartet, but there are only three Muppets on stage, two with bike horn noses and one with a desktop bell on his head. A quartet needs four. "Ah," says Big Bird, "but number four is coming." The audience hushes. "The Sesame Street Chamber Music Society is proud to present ... Yo-Yo Ma!"

A kindly looking, bespectacled man takes the stage. He wears a white shirt and bowtie, and carries a stringed instrument almost as tall as he is. With a furrowed brow and a smile, he draws a bow across the strings—and produces the most wonderful, joyful, yet sorrowful sound I have ever heard.

I am three years old and the cello has captured my heart. It isn't just the instrument's sound; it's also the tapestry of the four musicians weaving their individual parts together to create a whole. To this day, I remember the pure power of it. I didn't just hear the music. I *felt* it, deep inside. And somehow I knew, even then, that music was my true language.

*

Perhaps music was in my DNA. My mother majored in classical saxophone at Queen's University in Kingston, ON, Canada. She studied music theory, harmony, and history, and loved composing, arranging, and performing in ensembles. She had just broken up with her high school sweetheart when, in third year university, she met my father—a 6'3" Dane—at a local restaurant and wine bar that featured live music. He was an officer in the Canadian army, completing a course at the neighboring Military College. He had a good singing voice and appreciation for music. He walked her home and they were engaged before my mother graduated.

After getting married my parents traveled, both for my father's work and for pleasure. I was conceived in Damascus, Syria, where they lived for a time, but while my mother was pregnant they moved again, this time to Lahr, Germany, where my father had been posted. Six weeks after my birth, he was sent on a trip for work, leaving my mother alone with baby me. It was just the two of us, and she later told me she would talk and sing to me when we weren't napping. She was 24 years old.

Since a military salary was designed to support wives and children, my mother didn't have to work. But she loved music and was soon teaching students saxophone, flute, and clarinet from home. Some of my earliest memories are the sounds of her teaching in the living room of our apartment, the patient tone of her voice alternating with the deep and breathy honks of her beginner alto sax students. She had multiple students, and one was named Spencer. I thought that his saxophone harness looked like suspenders. When I was a little older, my father would take me for outings on Saturdays while my mother taught. My parents' marriage would not last, and later in life I often wondered if music served the same function for my mother as it did for me; if she too found she could escape difficult situations by playing, singing, creating music, and inspiring that gift in others.

My mother was my first piano teacher. We always had a piano in the house, even in Germany. There are photos of me as a baby and toddler, stretching up to reach the keys. When I was ready, my mother sat with me and taught me my first pieces from *Teaching Little Fingers To Play*. I still remember many of those little tunes.

I also loved to sing. I attended a German kindergarten (I spoke German as well as English), where singing songs together was an important part of the curriculum. At home I would absorb any music I heard. My father sang in The Lahr Police Choir for a while and would sing to me in Danish. He bought me little books of Danish children's songs and lullabies. To this day, I can sing the melodies and recall the words to those Danish songs phonetically. I have always been able to pick up songs and melodies easily by ear. I don't just hear music, it *enters* me, stirring my core and infiltrating my psyche.

When I was three and a half years old we moved to Ottawa, Canada, where my brother Pete was born. My mother continued to teach, and in addition to piano lessons (which I would continue until I was 16), I picked up Suzuki violin for a year. At home I listened to cassettes of the children's stories *Beethoven Lives Upstairs* and *Mr. Bach Comes to Call*. I would make up little songs about friends, people in the neighborhood, or the music students who came to the house. My brother and I also got a kick out of making up alternate underwear-themed lyrics to the Suzuki repertoire. I would later join our United Church junior choir on Sundays (with the promise of going out for lunch after practice!). In elementary school I sang in music class and school assemblies. I relished quiet reading or writing time, when our teacher would play ambient piano music on the cassette player. The music set a serene mood, profoundly affecting the class. While listening I felt instantly comforted, held, and at peace.

But music gave me something more. It began to suggest that I had something special to contribute to the world. In second and third grades in Kingston (where we moved when I was six) I continued to play the piano and a little recorder. I began to develop a sense of self-confidence, ownership, and identity with playing music, which I declared with a purple sweatshirt that read "Music is My Life." In my third-grade public speaking assignment I told the audience, "I play the piano, the recorder, and the fife, and will learn to play the cello when I get even *more* advanced in piano." At age seven I asked for cello lessons. Music gave me self-esteem and promoted a sense that I was different and unique.This sense continued to grow throughout my teens and beyond. At times it sustained me and at others it tormented me, depending on what was going on in my inner and outer worlds.

My enchantment with the cello was unrelenting. My mother would take us to all kinds of concerts: children's concerts, local high school musical productions, *The Nutcracker*, and even the local symphony. I always listened for the cellos at these concerts and in the recordings that matched the musical books we had. I'll never forget going to see the symphony perform Carl Orff's "Carmina Burana." The power and warmth of the cello section overwhelmed me: the cellos sang with the upper strings, rumbled with the basses, and blended seamlessly into the orchestra and chorus. The sound enveloped me and left me floored.

*

The summer I was eight years old, my mother, brother, and I attended a Suzuki Institute, a family summer music camp where we took lessons and participated in workshops. It was wonderful. One of the most powerful memories I have is singing with my mother and brother in a choir called Family Chorus. Our voices and equal roles united us, and through the medium of music our spirits merged. We were a family, a community, a clan. I realize now how important that sense of community is in childhood. I knew that no matter what challenges we faced, music could connect us and bring us together.

During our time at the Institute my mother and I visited a Suzuki cello class. There the teacher sat me down with a cello and checked me for sizing so that we could find the right-sized instrument for me before I began lessons. I was over the moon.

It wasn't just the sound of the cello that I loved. It was everything about it! I loved the different colors that cellos came in, from cheerful gold and fiery, flaming reds to a deep, warm brown. I loved the cello's size and presence; I loved how my knees hugged the wide lower bouts and my ribcage held up the cello's shoulders. When I cradled it between my knees it shielded my entire torso. It was like wearing a suit of armor. I could hide safely behind it, but in being a part of me it made me even stronger. I could thrive under my cello's protection and it gave me a voice and a backbone. I loved how it required my entire body to play, as if the sound was coming out of the deepest core of my being. It led to a feeling of both strength and safety. The curling f-shaped sound holes were elegant and beautiful. I loved how the instrument's neck rested beside mine and how the spiral scroll seemed to watch over my shoulder.

Not long after I got sized at the Institute, an ad went up on the public chalkboard at the Queen's University School of Music for three-quarter-sized student cello. My mom and I went to take a look. The woman who owned it said it had been sitting in a closet and hadn't been played for years. Inside the musty canvas case was a beautiful, shining, nut-brown cello, the perfect size for a young musician. It became mine!

CHAPTER 2

A Cellist

I adored Wolf Tormann, my first cello teacher. He was a handsome German who would teach me and mentor me for the next 14 years. While my adoration of him was unflinching, he terrified me at times. Once, when I was about 10, he pointed to a dusty, riveted old cello case in the studio closet that looked like a coffin and joked, "That's where you go if you don't practice!"

When it was obvious I hadn't practiced—sometimes for weeks—he wasn't impressed. I would feel ashamed and misinterpret his disappointment to mean that *I* was bad. How well I played the cello quickly became a reflection of my worth as a person, and if I played poorly and didn't practice, I felt worthless, pathetic.

I also didn't want to disappoint my musician mother, who was always on my case to practice. I hated being nagged, but still refused to do the work. So, there were battles and consequences. Bows and pencils were my projectiles; she lobbed back threats, bribes, and time negotiations. Privileges were revoked. Playdates and favorite TV shows were missed.

In the long, guilty days leading up to my cello lessons, I'd feel pangs of dread, compounded by feelings of inadequacy and being overwhelmed with new material. Just getting the instrument out of its case felt like climbing Mount Kilimanjaro.

When I would finally sit down and begin to play, I was instantly self-conscious. My mother would holler from the kitchen, "*What was that note?! Watch your tuning!*" or "Try that note *again!*"

I would scream back, "You don't even *know* what I was supposed to be doing! I was supposed to be working on the *rhythm*, not the *notes!*"

I started practicing just to save my own skin in my lessons. When my meagre efforts got an impressive reaction out of my teacher, I was thrilled and started practicing more regularly to keep him happy. Sometimes, to my delight, I was rewarded with Smarties or a Mars bar (my favorite!) for good work. Practicing, in turn, began to make *me* happier too, because I was developing my skills and getting more enjoyment out of playing the instrument.

My teacher noticed that I picked things up quickly and would give me new challenges and more advanced pieces to push me. I found joy in making progress and delighted in impressing him and my parents. My confidence really soared when I began to master vibrato, that subtle yet pulsating rapid variation of pitch that warmed and enriched my sound. It allowed me to truly express the music the way it was meant to be heard. "*Beauuutiful!*" my mother would holler when I played with vibrato.

When my teacher eventually told me that I was really a cellist, I beamed with pride.

*

When I was 10 years old, I auditioned for—and got into—a local string ensemble. I was thrilled to tell my Grade 5 teacher that I was joining the Junior Strings Orchestra! (I added "orchestra" to make Junior Strings sound more impressive.) Playing in a group with other cellists, violinists, violists, and bassists gave me a new way to be creative with my instrument and to explore new sounds. It also made me a stronger musician, and I got another huge confidence boost by being one of the best players in my tiny cello section. I was proud of our little concerts, where I would get to wear a special white lace blouse, a gift from my godmother. Sometimes a family member would even bring me flowers!

After a couple of years I heard that the more advanced local youth orchestra was looking for cellos. I successfully auditioned, a big stepping stone for a Grade 7 student. I felt extra special, being one of the youngest members of the group and hanging out with high school students. I loved it when the conductor pointed to the cellos and had us work on our part separately. I also loved sitting in my seat behind my cello, balancing the scroll on my forehead and daydreaming while the conductor rehearsed the brass or wind sections. There was so much stimulation: I was surrounded by an orchestra, making music with like-minded players, being a part of a team, and meeting new friends and boys—musician boys!

I met a double bass player in youth orchestra. He had red hair that grazed his chin. He was 18; I was 16 with a steady drummer boyfriend, but no matter. He was slouching against the school lockers when I bounced over to say hello to him before our first rehearsal of the season (I was totally gregarious—the endearing side of my early bipolar symptoms). He looked up and dourly told me his name. Graham. There was nothing to suggest that he was interested in talking to me or that he found me enchanting, but something about him piqued my curiosity.

In the orchestra our instruments were our identities and showcased our personalities. The brass musicians were party animals. The violinists were proper and a little tightly wound. The double bass players were cool, jazzy, and cute. And the cellists were laid back. As a musician, I had a place in the world.

But not everyone understood where music and I fit. When I was in eighth grade French immersion, I needed extra help in math and was tutored after school by my sciences-oriented teacher. I wasn't her favorite student, being wacky and artsy and sporting an Ani DiFranco nose ring. One day, exasperated by my math incompetence, she asked me what I imagined myself doing with my life. I replied quietly, "I want to be a musician ... I really want to be a cellist."

"And *what* on earth ..." she paused, darkly, "are you going to do with *that?*"

*

When I was 14 and had been learning cello for five years, my teacher gave me a heartfelt pep talk. If I worked really hard and got serious, he said, I could become good—really good. My natural musicality had to be nurtured by hard work, and if I didn't nurture it, it wouldn't happen. I took his remarks to heart. My cello playing improved dramatically once I learned how to practice effectively, working *slowly* in detail instead of rushing through my pieces beginning to end. I started playing from the J.S. Bach *Cello Suites* and practiced Saint-Saëns' *"Cello Concerto in A minor"*—my very first concerto—a difficult, virtuosic solo piece designed to be played with an orchestra.

I began at the very back of the cello section in youth orchestra, but year after year I worked my way up, and in Grade 11 and 12 I was principal cellist. I even got to play a double cello concerto by Vivaldi with my stand partner. We were the soloists, backed up by the entire orchestra. The experience was delicious: I *owned* the stage and the spotlight. In photos of that performance I am beautiful and glowing in my professional black attire and wild dreadlocks. I was Queen of the world. Our orchestra clothing, which united us like a school uniform, always gave me a sense of honor and pride. I loved "dressing up" to perform, and still do. I was so proud of my cello playing. It embodied who I was; it gave me my identity.

It was in high school that I started to learn how to really, *really* express myself, and my teacher noticed. My mother noticed. Everyone noticed. I was able to play my pieces the way I heard them in my head, closer than ever to emulating the professional recordings I listened to. I was also becoming aware of the special connection I had developed with my cello: I could channel the music and any emotion or thought I wanted to convey. I needed only to conjure it in my mind for it to be so. My gift was mysterious and oh, so precious to me.

The cello became *my* voice. When my emotions were all over the map, the cello reined me in and allowed me to channel my feelings through my playing. Again and again I would listen to recordings of my favorite cello pieces, like Shostakovich's "Cello Sonata in D minor" or Elgar's "Cello Concerto, Op.85." They would move me to tears nearly every time. I learned that being a cellist did not bind me to the classical tradition. I loved jamming with the Dave Matthews Band-influenced guitar players at high school coffee houses, and I loved listening to all-cello rock bands like Apocalyptica and the all-female Rasputina, with their Victorian corsets and poetry.

I told my mother that if she *really* wanted to punish me, the worst thing she could possibly do was take away my cello lessons with Wolf. I felt like he could really see me in ways that were, at times, impossible for my parents to appreciate. With him, I could open up and talk about what was really going on in my life. And sometimes I would just cry.

"You are so emotional," he would say. "You need an outlet. You know, playing your instrument can be an outlet." I anxiously fretted and confided in him about my struggles with my parents, who wanted me to control and contain myself and "pull up my socks." I once said I felt pressure from them to become a school teacher or lawyer instead of a musician. "I'm sorry," he replied, "but you would make a terrible lawyer! You are too sensitive!"

Playing the cello became complicated. It was an outlet for my energy, a vehicle for my creativity, a place where I could be completely free. It also tormented me. When I didn't practice I filled up with self-loathing, and I agonized that no matter how hard I worked, it would never be enough. I would never be enough. It was my sorrow, anguish, and the entrance to a bottomless pit where I was never enough, no matter how hard I strived. My talent imposed great responsibility on me, too. Despite my musical successes and achievements in many subjects, I felt enormous pressure. There was pressure from my parents and teachers to always aim higher and do *more*, pressure from society and the media to be beautiful, pleasant and thin, and pressure from myself to be perfect. Good was never good enough. While the expectations placed on me were very real, what I didn't realize was that my growing anxiety and spinning imagination were adding an unbearable weight to them—an excess that would eventually prove too much.

CHAPTER 3

Holding It In

Guatemala. My fifth birthday. I whack a gigantic Minnie Mouse piñata to celebrate. We go to the market where I balance mini bananas on my head like the other girls. I am with my 16-year-old newly adopted sister, who has smooth cocoa skin and wears an embroidered off-the-shoulder dress. She is stunning. Together, we belt out "Feliz Navidad," a song I hear everywhere. There is new music in Guatemala, and I like it. My new sister teaches me words in Spanish and shows me how to make tortillas.

We are in Guatemala visiting my father, who has been posted here. He tells us he found my new sister living in a dirt-floor shack in Honduras. Her family is big and poor, so we are bringing her home to help my mother and give her a better life in Canada. Sometimes I go with my father to take groceries to hungry children on the street. We tiptoe around sleeping bodies and put the bags down by their heads. He tells me they are needy, like my new sister.

We were bouncing around a lot in those days—from Ottawa to Guatemala, then Toronto, and later back to Ottawa. Shortly after the adoption my mother, brother, new sister and I flew back to Canada, while my father stayed behind. We four got along fine.

My sister seemed like a good helper for my mother, and she was a longed-for older sibling for me and my brother.

Then my father returned home, and everything changed.

That year my parents divorced. My mother took me and my brother and left. Our adopted Honduran sister stayed with my father. I saw her only once or twice more, and then never again.

This family upheaval affected everything, naturally. After staying with our grandparents briefly, Mom, Pete and I moved to a low-income housing complex in Ottawa. Now a single mother with two little kids to support, my mother realized she'd better find a career. She taught saxophone, flute, clarinet, and piano students at home while volunteering at schools and working toward a degree in education. Despite the little we had, she continued to teach me piano and managed to give me a year's worth of Suzuki violin lessons. That, and a home filled with music. Even the Disney movies we watched were full of songs; I loved pretending to be a mermaid and singing along. I was extremely sensitive and aware of what was going on in the family and between my parents, but I worked hard not to show it. I kept playing music and singing songs, showing everyone that I was okay.

It worked. Adults praised me for being such a pleasant and well-behaved little girl with sterling military manners. "Always so positive!" they would exclaim, and I would beam, happy to please them and maintain my reputation. I remember slipping *hard* on a cottage dock and landing flat on my face with a smack. Instead of allowing myself to cry as the adults gasped, I jumped up. "Never felt better!" I chirped. I had always been good at holding in pain, sadness, and fury. Now I became expert at it.

*

I was a good student when it came to detecting other people's needs. With diligence and skill, I studied the cues around me and mastered their varied meanings. I also became an expert in suppressing my own physical needs, in addition to stifling my emotions. I would frequently hold in the urge to urinate until the last possible second, closing my eyes and willing it away even when I doubled over in pain. My habit of repeatedly ignoring my body's signals later resulted in frequent urinary tract infections. Eventually I had to retrain myself to pee on time, which continues even to this day. Not knowing what was really going on, my mother praised me for being "a little camel."

On many joint-custody visits, my brother and I would dine out with my father. I dreaded being asked "Where would you like to *go*?" and being put on the spot. My mind would go blank, and I'd name a familiar place just so I didn't have to think or rock the boat. My father was a strict, military-type, old-school Scandinavian. Anyone near him was instantly at his command. He could also be warm and funny, and he'd sweep you off your feet with his charm. Early on I learned to never, ever cross him. At the restaurant our father would talk at us intensely about things like European politics or military warfare, while Pete and I nodded blankly like bobblehead dolls. His questions felt like demands, his explosive voice like a barking in my ears.

I would be full after a few bites of my meal, but I was too afraid to speak up or seem ungrateful by not finishing, so I would continue to eat until food slid back up my esophagus. When I was volun-told that I wanted dessert, I'd chirp, "Yes please!" and continue to eat in quiet agony, all the while ignoring my growing urge to pee. At the last possible moment I'd nervously excuse myself to the restroom. I would count how long my bladder finally took to empty, then fall to my knees and vomit into the toilet. Then I'd return to the table as if nothing had happened and finish my dessert like a good girl.

When I was seven our father married a wonderful woman who was half Korean, half Filipina. In the beginning we were told to shake her hand and ordered to hug her, but eventually we warmed up on our own and came to adore her. She made us feel safe during our visits, even when my brother's fussing once made her so cross that she didn't speak to us for days. We could truly relax around her.

On one visit to my father when he was posted in Norway, Pete and I noticed that his wife wasn't there. We snooped around and found that her Celine Dion CD's were gone. So were her cosmetics and hair elastics and her tiny vintage red car, Blossom. Nobody told us what had happened, and we pretended to ignore the huge elephant in the room. But her disappearance confused and frightened us. We knew that she had loved us and we missed her desperately. For years afterward, she appeared vividly in my dreams. I would see her in shopping malls, candy stores and parking lots. When I was out in public I would see a tall, slender Asian lady walk by and, thinking it was her, would call out her name. Later, when I moved to Toronto for grad school, I looked for her—but neither my brother nor I ever saw her again.

Many years later my father met a lovely 40-something-year-old accountant from Shanghai. When she gave birth to a boy named Alexander, it wasn't just me and Pete anymore. Alex's arrival cemented his mother as a genuine member of our family. Alex's birth introduced hope and promise, and the possibility of strengthening our relationship with our father. Alex also brought my father a level of vulnerability that, as a child, I would never have thought possible.

CHAPTER 4

Safe and Sound

When I was six my mother reconnected with her high school sweetheart, Bruce, the man she had broken up with before meeting my father. Bruce, whom we lovingly nicknamed "Bu," was in love not only with my mother, but also with Pete and me. We moved from our low-income townhouse in Ottawa to Bu's bungalow in Kingston, where my brother and I would grow up. Bu had a steady job as an engineer and my mom started working as a supply teacher (she would go on to become a teacher—a music teacher, too—and later a principal). Finally—a stable, loving, long-term home!

How lucky we were to grow up in a nice house with a pool, with summer camps, sports, and music lessons! We had nice parents who had jobs and loved us. What reason did we have to be sad, anxious or afraid? Other kids had it worse, way worse, and we were fine.

Just fine.

Yes, on the surface, my brother and I were fine. We had also become highly skilled at abusing each other. Biting was my first choice. It started with snapping at a whiny kid in my first-grade class to shut her up, but her tattling had me searching for other outlets. My brother was an excellent alternative victim. Once I bit him so hard that I left a deep, red-purple starburst on his shoulder. I was in deep trouble when my mother saw it. She screamed about a teacher seeing the mark and calling Children's Aid. (I later graduated to biting the lips of aggressive lovers who made me kiss them or forced me to comply while I inwardly protested *no, no, no* … This defense followed me through my twenties, and I was lucky I only broke the skin once.)

When it came to hand-to-hand combat, beating up my younger brother provided me with a feeling of sick relief. My musical ear relished the contrast as he went from red and screaming to purple and silent while I choked him. To me it was like slowly shutting off a spewing, sputtering faucet. I yearned to kill him and ominously fantasized about permanently destroying him with my own hands. My anger couldn't be contained any longer.

In retaliation, Pete would charge at me with large dining room chairs, kitchen knives, or a heavy, hard plastic toy dinosaur, swinging it by the neck like a club. I would slam and lock the bathroom door while he heaved his puny body against it and poked blades underneath.

When my brother wasn't around and I couldn't contain the rage inside of me, I hit and kicked our beloved Australian Shepherd, watching her flatten her ears and skulk away from me, weeping afterward when I realized what I had done, our trust broken.

I learned to get what I wanted by stealth so that I didn't rock the boat by asking the adults around me. I had zero boundaries. I stole socks from my stepdad's drawer to make my own toys and looted my mother's dresser. I rooted through other people's bathrooms and helped myself to their exotic products and toiletries. At school I snuck bites of cookie from a stash in my desk. I stole my brother's candy, treasures, and hard-earned pocket change. I also extorted money by promising to share the true meaning of the f-word. To maximize my profits, I invented additional f-words.

"FINKYDOODLE!" Pete would scream during a temper tantrum, hoping to shock our mother while I burst out laughing at the fool.

But all of this took energy. I startled and cried easily. Soon I was consciously working hard to keep myself together in public. Every night I would lie in my bedroom and sob for hours, watching the streetlamps project shadows onto my wall. My pain took on a voice.

Nobody loves you. Anyone who says they love you is lying. Someday, your parents will be dead. Everyone wishes you were dead.

Being told a simple "no" by a teacher—or anyone—paralyzed me with fear. My stomach would flop, my hands would shake, and I would feel weak in the knees. I had no clear sense of where others left off and I began.

Without personal boundaries, I was an easy target for predators. I was sexually assaulted on several occasions and became involved with boys far too early. And when I finally found the guts to tell someone, I paid a steep price.

When I was nine I was invited to my classmate "boyfriend's" 10th birthday pool party. Freckled and flat-chested, I was excited to show off my "sexy" new swimsuit, a tropical purple bikini with a flouncing mini skirt that layered over the bottoms. As I was frolicking in the pool, the boy dove under the water behind me, plunged his hand down the back of my bikini bottoms, jabbed between my legs and grabbed me in front, lingering as I tried to wriggle free. I was stunned, too horrified to scream. This was my punishment for wearing a tantalizing bikini. I carried on with the party activities, pretending to have fun.

At first I didn't dare tell a soul, but the violation was too traumatizing to keep to myself. To get it off my chest, I whispered what had happened to the boy's best friend on the school yard, who naturally told *everyone*. My story spread like wildfire. Kids I barely knew attacked me. They snarled that the boy would *never* do something like that, hissing, "How *dare* you spread lies about him!" The response was unbearable. There were no "Pink

Shirt Day" anti-bullying campaigns then, and my only escape was the girls' toilet stall, where I didn't have to hold back floods of tears.

Then, during one of many sleepless nights, I had a eureka moment: the perfect solution, a tool I would later refine to perfection and use to solve scores of future dilemmas.

I lied.

The next morning I blurted to my attackers that I had made a huge mistake. The incident never happened. It had actually been a vivid dream! My bad.

They bought it—I was safe. And wiser. Abuses followed— mostly friends, boyfriends—and I kept each one of them beautifully, perfectly to myself. I smiled on the outside and no one suspected the truth.

CHAPTER 5

Tumultuous Teens

I am 16. My grandmother has just given me a brand-new journal. In a burst of inspiration, I start a new page.

For school, for music, and for my general state of mind:

- *improve practice habits and diligence, at least two 45-minute sessions per day*
- *take dance and / or Pilates, as well as indoor soccer for fitness —maintain a healthy weight of 125 lbs*
- *write up a resume to keep adding on to*
- *work hard enough to get my average high enough for Queen's University*
- *get my G2 driver's license in May*
- *take my boyfriend out for a picnic :)*
- *get my rabbit neutered*
- *plan or make my formal dress (maybe after Christmas?)*
- *get more sleep*
- *go rock climbing*
- *save allowance in the bank (to increase $$)*
- *call Christine re. that CD*

• get together with friends
• make out with [my boyfriend] in a photo booth
• [have a] jam session with anyone who will!
• buy a huge, chunky sweater
• start taking a camera with me wherever I go :)
I will continue the habit of writing. It's good for my mental health ...

You know? I have way too many ideas. These creative ideas just keep popping into that silly head of mine, and often distract me from the task at hand. This is sort-of good, because I like fulfilling my creative intentions by ways of writing, playing, painting, sketching etc. but there is just no time ... Geez, I gotta start writing this stuff down. You can tell I have a lot to say, can't you?

As a teenager I sometimes felt every possible emotion at once: ecstasy and sorrow, euphoria and fury. It felt as though magical, transcendent powers were coursing through me. I viewed my entire existence as overflowing with supernatural ability, and I was certain that I was enchanted, gifted, special. When I closed my eyes my thoughts would flash across the screen of my eyelids, fleeting, flicking images with background music on repeat. Even my rock collection seemed magical.

It was often too much to bear, being able to feel so much at once. Sometimes it would spew out of me in angry, irritable, snapping outbursts where I lost all control (early symptoms that would follow me into adulthood). Overwhelmed by my racing mind at night, I would sit up in bed and purge free-fall streams of consciousness into my journal. My pen was a conduit, draining my disturbing thoughts.

I painted, too. I was enrolled in a specialized visual arts program where the art room, surrounded by huge windows, was filled with easels, drafting tables, and endless shelves of art supplies. A few weeks into the program we began our first project in oil painting. I wanted to paint what it *felt* like when I played the cello, the warmth of electricity that coursed through me when I made music. I wanted to paint the overwhelmingly beautiful tone I could produce when everything was working.

Using an old photograph of me practicing in a Halloween angel costume, I created an enormous self-portrait. Using thick gobs of paint, I upgraded the image. My smooth tresses became bouncing dreadlocks, springing off the canvas and encircled by real, wooden beads. With a palette knife I spread thick, buttery stripes of alizarin crimson and cadmium yellow, radiating outward from my cello and the golden glow of my skin. The rich hues melted together and surrounded my figure, conveying the sonorous, glowing tone of my instrument and the joy that it brought me when I played, the light that shone when the curtain of darkness lifted. My gift.

I painted Edward Elgar's "Cello Concerto in E minor." Its traumatic opening chords were crimson swells. The winds that echoed the heart-wrenching melody were watercolor blues and ocean grays. My brush saturated the paper, tearing a soft pulpy hole as I lost myself to the music, filling sheet after sheet with color. I was enamored by the concerto and the young British cellist Jacqueline du Pré. Over and over I would watch her passionate performance in Christopher Nupen's black-and-white documentary *Jacqueline du Pré and the Elgar Cello Concerto*. I was haunted by the fact that multiple sclerosis claimed her at the height of her career. The tragedy of her death allowed me, just for a moment, to put my own struggles into perspective.

I hate my looks. I can never make up my mind. I hate the fact that no matter what I do it's never good enough for my workaholic mother. I hate the way I'm oversensitive; I hate that I don't fit in. I hate my constant need for love and acceptance. I hate the burden I bring on the world around me. I hate those days where my confidence is so low I just want to die so someone might remember me. I hate the way I try my best at almost everything I do but wind up getting shit on because why would anyone notice anyway? I'm either too uptight, too easy going, too stuck up or immature. I'm sick of trying, I'm sick of living, I'm sick of trying to please the world. I'm sick of all this goddamn pressure to be perfect and I'm sick of having short

dirty fingernails and a potbelly. I hate myself and I am afraid of
the woman I am to become ...

On the outside I was perky, charming, right as rain, and eager to please. Inside I fought secret battles, and I often exploded behind closed doors. A threatening presence would overwhelm me. My darkness, like a black cloud, would cover me from head to toe like a weighted blanket. Negative thoughts would flood my spinning brain, and a sense of hopelessness and guilt would paralyze me. My entire existence felt worthless. I was nothing but a masquerading impostor, an utter failure, undeserving of every one of my talents and privileges.

I would often have a hard time concentrating in class, and my marks showed it. I suffered wretched crying fits in the privacy of my bedroom, where I had madly covered the walls, from floor to ceiling, with magazine cut-outs. I would scream into damp pillows as silently as I could, punch my face and body, and pull my long hair. I beat myself for being stupid, lazy, ugly, fat, pathetic, and *never good enough*.

My mother often accused me of "gallivanting around" with boyfriends, and my lying skills were useful when I wanted to appease her or avoid arousing suspicion. I would tell her that I was "at a friend's house" when, in fact, I had been off with a strange guy other than my regular boyfriend. At one point I had a terrifying pregnancy scare that left me sobbing through my piano lesson. The stress made my period even later. My scare transformed into a shame storm of self-hate—I hated myself for being promiscuous, too "experienced," and utterly broken. As a self-punishment I would subject myself to physical abuse and tell myself repeatedly that I was a worthless slut with no reason to live. I felt completely unworthy of love. I lied about my bruises the next day.

I would eventually graduate to scratching my wrists—I was too chicken to cut deeply—and I would numb myself with stolen alcohol. After bouts of overeating, I would shove my fingers down my throat, heaving until I vomited. My righteous absolution. I was flooded with destructive thoughts, particularly fantasies of my own death.

I didn't share the depths of what I was going through with my parents, and they struggled to understand. I was routinely told how common it was to have "normal ups and downs," and I was reminded over and over again of how privileged and lucky I really was. How many other kids get cello lessons and have a pool? Other kids from split families had to visit their dads every other week. I only had to go once in a while. My mother, mostly in the dark about my misery, repeatedly quipped perkily, "Yup! You're normal. Totally normal. Normal "ups and downs"!" I'm not sure who she was trying to convince—me or herself. She would also say, "This, too, shall pass!"

But I had a haunting suspicion that my experiences were something other than "normal," and that they may be here to stay.

Luckily, my family doctor had the wisdom to check in beyond my physical health, even in the late '90's. She was safe to talk to. After I opened up at age 15 about my frequent bouts of sadness and despair, my feelings of worthlessness and trouble sleeping and concentrating in class, she looked into my eyes and asked, "Did you know that your mother is *extremely* proud of you?"

Yeah right! I was confused, feeling unworthy of even the slightest praise. After listening to my symptoms, my doctor explained to me that I had a chemical imbalance in my brain, so she prescribed Prozac, an SSRI (selective serotonin reuptake inhibitor) for depression.

Depression. At the time the label made perfect sense, and my symptoms seemed to fit it. Not only that, but all teenagers experience some depression during their "normal ups and downs," so I was perfectly normal, just like Mom promised. I agreed to take Prozac and at the time thought it must be the answer.

Taking Prozac was bittersweet. It seemed to even me out and keep me safe, but I was in turmoil nonetheless, feeling as though my sparkling creativity and exuberant energy had been sucked out of me. I felt flat. I developed a prejudice against taking drugs, and my attitude was reinforced by my high school sweetheart, who was also medicated and despised "the drugs." We were influenced by the Britpop bands that we listened to, especially songs like "The Drugs Don't Work" by The Verve.

Furthermore, taking drugs shattered my mother's promise to me that I was perfect and normal. I felt weak, damaged, and broken for needing to depend on medication, but I was trapped: the fear of relapse loomed if I stopped.

Around the same time that I received my first prescription for antidepressants, I started seeing a counsellor. Talking to someone in a safe space—someone devoted to me with no personal agenda—was *powerful*. I floated out of her office after each session. For the very first time I felt truly listened to and heard. As a result of counselling I became more insightful and increasingly self-aware. I was starting to untangle all of the different threads of the tapestry that made up my life, determining which ones belonged to me and which ones really belonged to someone else. (I would later seek similar therapy throughout crises in university and graduate school, searching for a "healthy adulthood," not knowing I was treating something else.) Still, I struggled with the idea of having to rely on daily medication. Yes, I had been accepted into our town's best fine arts program and I was painting, writing, and playing music, but my creative spirit felt like it was ebbing away, and I thought I had no business being in the program any longer.

In retrospect, I am glad that I didn't quit my fine arts program. My high grades contributed to my acceptance into Queen's University during the competitive "double cohort year," when Grade 13 was discontinued in my province (this meant that Grade 12 and Grade 13 students—double the applicants—applied to university in the same year). At the time, however, I felt that I had bottomed out and lost the connection to the light that made me vital, alive, special, and unique. Believing that my creativity was gone made me more depressed. The thought that I was not the same person I used to be was scary and unbearable.

I started my last year of high school with the best of intentions, but struggled to keep up with my own expectations. I was under a great deal of stress and increasingly overwhelmed with all of my activities, since I had to excel and be the best in all of them. I was in a pressure cooker of my own making, and the build-up of steam was straining the lid.

Red face, puffy eyes, double chin, facial hair, unibrow, potbelly, fat arms, stubby legs, bloating, cramps, greasy hair, no makeup, stained white t-shirt, garish pink sneakers, teeth unbrushed, tea breath, stubbly armpits, hangnails, calloused fingertips, frontal extreme thong wedgie, mossy teeth, runny nose, ingrown hair, falling pants, exposed butt crack, 3 tummy rolls, droopy breasts, dry skin, weird hair, overtiredness, malnourishment, could I be any uglier today?? I FEEL like an April Fool!!

... Gaah midterms, studying, practicing for audition on Saturday, practicing for soccer, practicing for concerto in May, memorizing for Canadian Music Competition = overeating, overtiredness, overstress, over-frustration from lack of intimacy, over-broke from over-laziness and overspending habits.

What really ailed me was beyond the reach of Prozac. On top of having an undiagnosed serious mental health condition, my inner life was still an amalgam of attitudes and behaviors that I had adopted while being unaware of their origin or how serious my condition was. I suffered visceral, repeated visions, images and dreams of my own medieval execution and being tortured and murdered. I fantasized, especially at night, about ending my own life. Would I hang myself like others? Cut my wrists in the bath? The idea of walking into traffic was seductively appealing. If I couldn't be perfect, what good was there in carrying on? I decided that my only chance of being loved or remembered was if I were dead. *That would show everyone*, I thought.

I still worshipped my cello teacher and was hugely invested in making him happy. My precarious self-worth was mixed up with musical performance. Playing the cello could still make me feel special, extraordinary, and unique, but if a performance didn't go as well as I had hoped, I felt like trash.

One terrible day, I had a horrible fight with my boyfriend followed by a devastating cello lesson where I was ill prepared and emotional. My teacher was not impressed. Feeling wretched and ashamed pushed me under, and I slipped below the surface. I was worthless. I had let everybody down: my parents, my teachers, my boyfriend, everyone. I had hit rock bottom. Convinced that the world would be a better place if I simply removed myself from it, I swallowed a bottle of extra strength Tylenol.

But my plans for a grandiose exit failed. After a short hospital stay with no psychiatric evaluation, I was sent home. The overdose caused little more damage than muscle twitches and a sore liver.

CHAPTER 6

The Enthusiastic Egg Donor

Because of the high school focus programs I took, I managed to graduate near the top of my class and was accepted into Queen's University's Bachelor of Music program, where I would continue to study with Wolf Tormann.

While most students face a steep academic and social learning curve in first year, I took it to another level. I was wild and jacked up on *Sex and the City*. Still under the legal drinking age, I avoided being carded by frequenting grad clubs and brew pubs. Following yet another passionate fight with my high school boyfriend over Thanksgiving weekend, I chopped off my dreads and gave myself a pixie cut. He and I broke up and mended things a few more times, but it took a year and several episodes of deceit for things to really end. With the relationship over, I was even more carefree. I wore large, silver hoop earrings and dressed provocatively. I was routinely caught up in three or more romantic dramas. Men. Women. It didn't matter. I became an expert hunter who could identify and stalk sexual prey with precision.

I tried to be responsible and expected a lot of myself academically, yet missed exams and skipped or slept through classes. As a result, I ended up failing two courses. I pulled up my socks, but I continued to have trouble concentrating throughout my time at Queen's. I imagined that my classmates could sit through a lecture, passively absorb every detail, and hardly have to study, whereas I could not process a thing unless I sat right up front, took notes constantly, and scribbled and highlighted all over my textbooks. It didn't help that for two summers, after first and second year, I worked the night shift at Denny's, serving Grand Slams and Moon Over My Hammy to drunk customers between 11:00 pm and 7:00 am. The red-eye scheduling wreaked havoc on my already poor sleeping habits, and it created a routine that carried over into the school year, making it nearly impossible to be awake and focused for morning classes.

Halfway through second year, I started pursuing a leather-jacketed third year who had long red hair and played the double bass: Graham from youth orchestra. He was quiet, steady, and whip-smart. I badly wanted to impress him. I started to feel stupid for missing classes. I needed him to see that I was really bright, too. When we shared classes, I made myself sit at the front so I could astonish him with my exceptional concentration and note-taking skills. Some of our dates were true study dates, and under Graham's influence, my grades picked up. I even got competitive and was infuriated when he breezily turned down an offer to join a specialized performance program that had rejected me, even after I had worked my butt off. In my fourth year, I was finally accepted into that program.

I worked hard throughout my third and fourth years and my marks soared. I was principal cellist of the university orchestra, playing all the solos, and I enjoyed taking courses in jazz improvisation and avant-garde music. I was devouring Beethoven's "String Quartet Op. 59 No. 2" and Shostakovich's "String Quartet No. 8" with my chamber group, learning Edward Elgar's entire "Cello Concerto Op. 85" by memory and preparing a public graduating recital. I was hired to perform in the local symphony (Carl Orff's "Carmina Burana," which I had heard as a child) and in local theatre productions. I was told by my chamber coach that I would have great success in a career in music. I also had lessons with graduate school mentors who encouraged me to apply for a master's degree, and I taught eight private cello students. Outwardly I was fulfilled and accomplished, but inwardly ...

I have got to start controlling myself ... I need to take charge of what I want and quit being so damn lazy and doubtful.

I can wake up early to practice for a few hours. I can set time aside to exercise daily. I can stop giving in to sugary things. I can start drinking more water. I can get many things accomplished on a free day. I can stop spending so much. I can get to sleep before midnight. I can create a routine. I can get ahead for September ...

After convocating with a Bachelor of Music Performance (honors), my plan was to continue on to graduate school in cello performance. While working a data-entry job at my stepdad's company, I auditioned for a few graduate programs to no avail. I started to consider taking a year off, but the monotony of life in my workplace cubicle gave me time to scheme, and one day inspiration struck. I remembered a school that friends had attended and loved, one of the best, most competitive performance schools in the country: The Glenn Gould School at the Royal Conservatory of Music. Originally I had dismissed it, thinking I didn't stand a chance. But now a fearless, electric impulse swept through me and, feeling invincible, I emailed one of the school's top teachers. It was mid-summer and auditions had long passed, but the school agreed to audition me. My playing was in great shape from all the other auditions. And I was accepted!

With two weeks' notice I was moving to Toronto, the big city. And Graham was coming with me. He was touring the USA on electric bass with a Celtic rock band at the time, and he was thinking about going back to school. Once we'd moved he would apply to grad school in Toronto while I started my program. We moved into a spare room in his older sister's townhouse. It was spontaneous. Glorious. Madcap.

Graduate school started and I was soon busy learning new music for my classes, ensembles and orchestra, but I also got a part-time job as an orchestral strings specialist at a large music retailer. There I got to know local musicians, learn about the latest gear, and pick up gigs on the side. I also got private students when customers who were renting a cello were also looking for a teacher. Through my part-time job and handful of students, I earned enough to get by, but I was always on the lookout for a project that would engage my creativity and spirit and indulge my hunger for adventure. I kept an eye out for summer master class programs in the mountains, or really big gigs like the one where I performed live with Kanye West at the Air Canada Centre—twice—or when I was invited on a cross-Canada tour with a band called the Flowers of Hell.

One night after a shift at the store, I scoured a free monthly entertainment magazine. I'm not sure what I was looking for in the classified ads, but I often found things to jump on, such as concert tickets. What caught my eye that night, however, was the phrase "starting a family." Couples were advertising for egg donors. Now, there was an idea. Yes! Inspiration rushed over me, and my mind flooded with possibilities. I immediately responded to not one, but two egg donor ads, with a photograph and detailed explanation about how appealing my genes were. *This* was the project I'd been seeking. Yes. Yes. Yes!

No sooner had I begun feverishly researching egg donation in Canada than I received a reply from one of the couples. Days later I visited the fertility clinic to meet with a counsellor about my intentions, and I began an email relationship with the prospective parents. Each step and each meeting was positive, and every medical test came back with favorable results. I was over the moon. I was an ideal candidate and an exceptional human specimen. I now had detailed medical proof that my overall health was immaculate and completely normal—just like my mother had been telling me for years. And not a red flag in *sight* concerning my mental health!

I picked up my expensive kit of vials and syringes and began injecting myself daily in the stomach with fertility hormones to ripen my eggs to maturity. I commuted an hour downtown to attend 7:00 am monitoring appointments, where a condom-covered ultrasound wand was inserted daily to count the maturing egg follicles. I prepared to have my eggs harvested surgically by means of a needle through my vaginal wall and into my ovaries. I ran all over the city to appointments, ignoring Graham and my school commitments, and gushed about my shocking secret to trusted chamber music colleagues in my grad program. What a high! I was amazing—a saintly altruist, gifting to strangers my extraordinary genes that would soon enter the world.

I would help out another couple by giving them something that they needed, and I would pay things forward. Besides, I was young and healthy, in grad school, and years—maybe even a decade—away from needing my eggs. A brilliant idea.

On the day of my egg retrieval, I felt extra special when I learned that an unusually large number of eggs had been retrieved. Why expect less? My selfless gesture and my genes were exceptional, so there was no surprise that my eggs were too. But my ovaries were so sensitive that they had been hyperstimulated. I had developed ovarian hyperstimulation syndrome, a potentially dangerous condition that caused my abdomen to fill with fluid and required serious monitoring. Yet after the uncomfortable retrieval, I chirped out loud, "I would do it again in a heartbeat." I felt superior and saintly for putting myself through this enormous upheaval to help these people.

Sadly, none of the embryos from my egg donation resulted in a successful pregnancy.

CHAPTER 7

Higher and Higher

While working at the music retailer, I trolled the internet for auditions and gig opportunities under the guise of looking up customer accounts or doing online research. Flipping between *Orchestras Canada*'s job postings and Craigslist, I dreamed of finding a good audition opportunity in Ontario and winning a job. Classical performance majors are trained to win orchestra jobs, and I didn't feel like a "legit" musician without one. Finally I saw an ad for an orchestral position that looked like a good shot. It was 350 kilometers from my home, but no matter. My obsessive wheels were already spinning. I immediately sent my resume and eagerly awaited a reply. The orchestra's coordinator soon got in touch, and, in corresponding with him, I applied the same relentless drive that got me into graduate school. The orchestra's audition date gave me just the right amount of preparation time. I got to work right away, organizing orchestral excerpts from my library into a neat binder, studying the complex scores, and crafting my solo pieces by memory, bar by bar. I felt resentful that I had to work at the store, unlike other musicians who, I envisioned, were supported by wealthy relatives and lived in their parents' mansions.

Some mornings I would set an early alarm so I could practice in the store's tiny instrument trial room before the store opened at 9:30 am. To sneak in any practice I could during my shift, I would run through orchestral excerpts under the guise of testing store instruments. Between practices, I obsessed. Was I really good enough? Did I have a speck of a chance at an orchestra job? Ah, what was the point, anyway? Why waste the audition panel's time with my mediocrity? The audition invaded my mind, especially at night. Going to bed and closing my eyes turned on the familiar TV in my brain. I could watch the channels change for hours.

Under all of this self-imposed pressure, I became increasingly irritable and explosively reactive, just like when I was a teen. Practicing feverishly in the small living room of our apartment, I was concentrating on a difficult passage when my gentle Graham quietly approached from the side and whispered, "Darling ..."

"WHAT?" I screamed from behind my cello. "Why. WHY? Ohmigod. WHY ARE YOU HERE?!"

"I poured your tea."

Despite all the performing I had done, I still suffered bouts of performance anxiety. I would find myself in a state of fight-or-flight, my heart pumping, palms sweating, and limbs shaking. At times I would experience out-of-body sensations. I would look down at my own arm drawing the bow across the string, and suddenly my other hand would lose touch with where the notes really were. Sometimes I would blank out entirely while playing. "Your problems aren't physical, *they're mental!*" my graduate school teacher once observed.

While I was beginning to trust that the more I performed, the better I could cope with my nerves, I wasn't going to let them ruin this audition. So I got a prescription for beta blockers. "These pills are *grrreat,*" the elderly pharmacist assured me with a wink. And she was right. I tested one tablet on a low-pressure gig, downing it 40 minutes before the performance. Just like magic, my pounding heart, shaking arms, and confusion were all gone!

Early on the morning of my audition, Graham and I—armed with my cello—piled into a rental car and drove for four hours. I was buzzing with anticipation, ready to play my heart out. I arrived early and was directed to a small practice room, where I took my time warming up. I stayed energized with a pre-performance banana and popped my beta-blocker right on time. Forty minutes later I was sitting in the audition chair.

I drew my bow over the ringing steel cello strings and began. Everything—the planning, the hundreds of practice hours, my short fuse, the obsessive ruminating, the destructive thoughts, lashing out and pushing Graham away—all came down to this moment. This was the moment. There was nothing to do but play as beautifully as I knew I could. And I did.

In the interview that followed, I told the panel I would make the job work *no matter what*, by commuting from Toronto and somehow shuffling my 20 private students. I hadn't really worked out the logistics, but I knew I *wanted* that job. After an anxious wait, the executive director came to offer me the position. I was ecstatic and eager to yell, "YES YES YES!" but I could hear Graham's rational voice in my head, telling me to settle down and think about it before replying. I asked for a few days to consider the offer.

I was on cloud nine during the car ride home, flying high on my accomplishment. While I chattered away and marveled at my genius, the ever-logical Graham expressed skepticism about the logistics. He listed the reasons why taking this job made no sense and insisted that the pay was not worthwhile. I begged him, for just this moment, to let me enjoy my triumph.

But I couldn't say no, and I bulldozed every obstacle. The orchestra was in Sudbury, a four-hour drive in good weather. It was too expensive to buy a car and too dangerous to drive regularly at night and in the Northern Ontario winter. I investigated planes, trains, and rideshares, but the only feasible solution was the bus. So I accepted the position, quit my part-time job at the music store, and began a weekly five-hour bus ride to Sudbury and back. I expected my family to be just as excited about the opportunity as I was; after all, I had finally "made it" as a *legit* musician, with a professional orchestra job. But when they heard what the job entailed, they thought I was nuts. What did they know? I told myself. *This* was my big break.

My new position included teaching at the conservatory of music, and I expected to walk into a full studio. But most of the cello students had left to follow their teacher, who had resigned. So, with no contacts in Sudbury, I found myself starting a studio from scratch. No problem.

As my studio grew, I began staying overnight once a week. Fortunately the symphony's treasurer and his wife were kind and generous enough to billet me on Tuesdays and during concert weeks. But getting to work on Tuesdays meant scrambling out my door in Toronto, schlepping a cello and backpack on the city bus and subway to the coach terminal, and boarding the Ontario Northland bus that departed at 11:30 am.

My northbound seatmates were benign: seniors visiting friends, college students heading home, and the odd open-mouthed gum chewer. The friendly drivers would welcome my cello aboard as my travel companion. En route to Sudbury I studied orchestral scores or gazed out the window, watching concrete jungles and freeway gave way to lush forests and rivers before the barren moonscape of the Canadian Shield emerged with the white slivers of birch trees surrounding Ramsey Lake. At the end of the five-hour journey the driver would drop me between stops at the side of the road. From there, a ten-minute walk would me to the studio, with exactly five minutes before my first student arrived. The day was full. For dinner I scarfed a protein bar while rushing to evening rehearsal. Playing music and making art as a part of a team grounded me. After rehearsal I would hitch a ride to my billet and crash in the sanctuary of my bed. It all seemed worth it.

The next morning would be spent practicing alone in my studio before the first lesson. I knew enough about taking care of myself to escape to a yoga class or meet a colleague for coffee in my relatively free daylight hours. On my office floor, a green paisley dog pillow masqueraded as a decorative pouf. I used it for naps. I also kept a towel, sheets, and inflatable camping mattress in my closet, in case I had to sleep in the office overnight. After the last lesson of the evening I would pass the lonely period before my 1:00 am southbound bus by ordering a pizza, calling a taxi, and counting down the hours until I could crash in my real bed in Toronto at 5:30 am.

The 1:00 am homebound bus would be on the last stretch of its long journey from British Columbia, and it would usually be packed. I saw a breadth of humanity, and my cello and I were a part of it. Fragrant backpacking west-coast troubadours. Mennonite families armed with grocery bags full of Lucky Charms cereal and Wonderbread. Belligerent drunks. I even overheard drug deals being coordinated on payphones in the station, then the "businessmen" would hop aboard. We all had somewhere to be.

Taking my 1924 German cello aboard was a gamble, as it needed its own seat. Some drivers recognized me and, with a knowing wink, would allow me to stash my instrument up front, behind the driver's seat. But no matter how much I begged, other drivers forced me to consign it to the bumpy, unheated undercarriage, even at –20 degrees in the middle of winter. Pissed off, but not willing to make a bigger stink, I would spend the entire ride cringing at every bump and turn while my tuning pegs slipped beneath in the freezing cargo and all four strings unraveled in their peg box.

Finding a seat for my cello was a hassle, but finding a seat for myself was no small feat either. Passengers traveling across the country had often already made themselves at home, filling empty seats with stashed coats, purses and knapsacks, using them as a "taken" sign. They protected their territory with outstretched legs or by pretending to sleep. "Hi, excuse me," I would say. "May I sit here?" To my surprise, I often received varying responses of "no". As I shuffled my way to the back of the dark, creepy bus, I shuddered to think of whom I might end up beside. Whenever I had little choice but to sit beside a single man, I couldn't relax for fear of being assaulted or grabbed and I would be flooded by flashbacks. I would lean to one side, trying not to make contact with the "manspreader" whose knees were in my personal space. I'd stay awake, jolted and paranoid for the entire ride, ready to pounce if he so much as breathed on me. If he started friendly conversation, I was curt.

Some weeks I would travel up and back in the same 24-hour period so as not to miss a day of teaching in Toronto. I had lined it up near flawlessly so that not a single student or colleague would be put out. I felt like a hero for making it work. Despite more than half of my paycheck going toward transportation, I justified that it allowed me to maintain my big-city life and convinced myself that it made financial sense. To cope with the mounting stress, I self-medicated. I began taking *Rhodiola rosea*, a powerful herb that is said to increase energy and build resistance to stress and fatigue. I quickly got hooked. The herb helped, but it didn't eliminate the source of my problem.

*

As I was wrapping up my first season in April, my father's wife gave birth to my half-brother, Alexander. I wasn't sure how to navigate this new role—I was old enough to be his mother!—and without realizing it I reverted to my childhood pattern of trying to be perfect. Despite the insanity that was my schedule and commute, I took it upon myself to plan a baby shower in a city that was five hours away.

It was stressful to plan the event for Ottawa while living in Toronto and commuting weekly to Sudbury. To relieve some of the stress, I compulsively escaped to an antique store that specializes in expensive estate jewelry. There I dreamily tried on engagement rings. Modern solitaire diamonds were disenchanting, I mused. These rings had a story. May I see this one? Oh, what about that one? No, *that* one!

I found a ring I truly loved and impulsively put it on hold, along with a couple of others. I then told Graham. No pressure.

Poor guy. He was in grad school and this was coming out of nowhere. Despite being somewhat exasperated that I was all of a sudden looking at rings, he gave me the A-okay to pick one just before I jetted off for a whirlwind 24 hours to host the baby shower.

The symphony season had just ended for the summer, and I felt sad and stressed about leaving home again. I was upset at myself for seeming pushy, potentially rushing and ruining an organic, romantic gesture by Graham. As I stood on the sidewalk with my rolling suitcase, a sketchy white van slowed down and the driver leered. "Hey Chiquita, going on vacation?"

I was so furious I lost it, screamed expletives at him, and gave him the finger. When I finally got to the train station, I stopped in the sea of people, leaned against a pillar, and cried. I could no longer hold things in. I couldn't stop weeping in line, and I couldn't stop when I sat on the train. I felt guilty and miserable.

Finally, I called Graham. He reassured me. I wasn't being pushy and he told me not to worry. He was just about to call the antique store! So, on the train ride to Ottawa, I pored over images of the ring that I had saved to my phone.

Coming home, I was physically and emotionally exhausted from the pressures of hosting the shower. I stared out the window at the sunset and countryside and dreamed all kinds of things. I kept wondering about the engagement ring I had picked out at the antique shop. From time to time, I glanced down at the *Stone Diaries*. The characters in my book were getting married on the very page where my bookmark lay that evening—when Graham proposed to me in our little apartment.

CHAPTER 8

The Body Speaks

It was summer. I had just finished my first season with the orchestra, and my home-based schedule was full with teaching and gigging. Being stationary for an extended period of time in Toronto was a relief. But one night in August I woke to an intense, gripping pain right under my rib cage, as though a fist was clenching my gut. My first thought was a gallbladder attack. I struggled to sleep through the pain and in the morning, I did some research. I discovered that the common wisdom is that gallbladder attacks are often triggered by rich, fatty food, like heavy meats, creamy pastas, and fried foods. Sure enough, the previous night's dinner had consisted of ribs and fries. Suspecting gallstones, I called my doctor. While waiting for my appointment I experienced constant nausea and pain. My stomach felt walnut-sized, shrunken into a knot. I burped repeatedly and the acid burned my esophagus. Attempting any solid food made me want to vomit. I consumed liquids only and lost eight pounds in a couple of days. At this point, I was freaking out. Was I paying the price for one too many rich meals, or was my body indicating a bigger problem?

My doctor sent me for various tests, and I found myself drinking odd liquids and contorting into different positions to have my organs examined by ultrasound and X-ray. Then I received my diagnosis: gastroesophageal reflux disease, or GERD. I'd likely have it forever. I was prescribed Omeprazole, a drug that reduces the production of gastric acid. I resented the prescription. The change from only taking herbs or vitamins to daily medication felt like a huge step backward, just like the Prozac during my teenage years. I couldn't stand the idea of being reliant on drugs.

I researched my condition and learned that stress is linked to digestive and gastrointestinal problems. A fulsome understanding of my health was still in my future, but certain things began to make sense. I was taking the bus to get to a job five hours away, staying at a billet, traveling home through the night, eating poorly, and teaching students in between. I was chronically in a state of stress.

My first trip back to Sudbury for the next orchestra season was hard, but in a different way. I began to feel nauseated as soon as I started to pack my bags.

I am on a bus, headed to my "Northern Getaway." I have forgotten my debit card and birth control pills, and have been clenching my jaw and grinding my teeth at night, and getting frequent painful UTIs, but I am content and made it out for a jog again today. I have my noise-canceling headphones on, so I can take in the changing autumn leaves but block out the nearby passenger coughing fits.

*Yesterday, I impulse-purchased two new bridal magazines. The consumerism that a wedding inspires is incredible. I even blew $400 on six sessions of laser hair removal, just because "wouldn't it be nice to take care of it for the wedding and evermore?" Hope it is worth it! I do really need to tighten the purse strings, and I mean **really**! I also can't believe I am spending $1200+ tax to have my gown remade and altered. I should have asked what a new bodice would cost instead of blurting out that I had $1200 to spend.*

Considering changing my name, but I'm a performer!

I used my many hours on the bus to call vendors and plan our wedding on my laptop.

How am I going to keep doing what I am doing, and support or even have a family? The house, the playroom, the cute kid … am I cut out for it? Right now I am back and forth to Sudbury every week, coming home on the bus at 5:30 am Thursday mornings. It works on paper, but my healthy body is starting to suffer. Next Tuesday our wedding photographers are coming to our house to take our engagement photos! I just don't want to leave a great opportunity, but surely two years is enough.

I confided to my mother that I wanted to apply for teacher's college. She gleaned that I was tired of my exhausting commute to Sudbury and was using that plan as a way out. After years of pressuring me to have a blueprint for my life, she surprised me by saying, "Well. You don't *have* to have a plan." A few days later she sent me a text:

There is a Globe and Mail[2] *article you need to read, about Marcia Walker throwing out her law degree.*

Marcia was determined to be a lawyer. She hated the work but was determined to "stay on track," and telling people she was in law school was impressive. At the end of her first year, she had an out: she was pregnant with her son. She persevered. She told the bored, depressed, questioning inner voice to suck it up. She could have easily left law, but no way: that would have meant that she didn't know what she was doing, and she had a plan. Then another baby. Law school became a retreat from "the wailing and mucus of her living room." No quitting now—she was going to be a lawyer, damn it! It didn't matter that she didn't like the work. What mattered was staying on track. Her relationships suffered. She developed a chronic eye twitch …

Marcia Walker's essay unleashed a stream of consciousness from within me. In my journal, I poured out my turmoil.

In a way, I want to do my very best now, so I don't have kids too early and resent them for my not "making it" as a musician, and wasting the last years of my 20's.

Is trying to be the best cellist I can be making me hollow? I feel so fulfilled when I play and contribute to something bigger than myself though. Is that the same as being hollow?

I am in the arts, but look how much I work! See! I don't even take breaks, and I have no time or energy for friends! I must be successful, just like everyone wanted! I am just so busy! See?? I can make lots of money too, just like all of you, and I can do it playing the f*cking cello! I can do something completely different from you and earn a living, by being myself and playing beautifully and sharing that with others. Besides, everyone loves the cello.

Taking an art course would be the best ever. But I literally have no time or spaciousness to do it, plus, if I'm not working, I'm not making money, and if I am not doing that it means I am lazy and indulgent. No "lazy artist" here! If I work until I make myself ill, then I have done what I need to do. Maybe I can take a summer course.

Am I trying to impress people by pursuing my career? No, but I love that it impresses people—especially bigwig doctors and lawyers. They come to see me for guidance. They see me as a role model in how to make a living from pursuing your dreams. I am the proof that you can do this for a living. I am respected. Look how hard I have to work for some credibility! I might even buy a house with my teaching money! Then won't everyone be proud? And a musician nonetheless!

*When I focus on what I want, I will attract it. What you think about you bring about! I will use my tools of goal setting to get what I want in my performing, teaching and business life. Forget yesterday! If I want to have more, I need to **be** more. What does principal cellist and featured soloist look and act like? Make working my goals a habit. Consistency! Routine! Tortoise always wins?*

At times I felt direction and momentum, but really I was flailing around and sending my energy off in all directions. Not only was I reconfiguring my career and planning a wedding, I was preparing for a solo performance with the orchestra.

January 29. I am riding the bus to Sudbury, up for the whole week for our orchestra concert. It is the last concert before my own concert, as a soloist. I keep having ups and downs such as being so overwhelmed that I can't practice or get any work done. Or sometimes I just well up and cry for no reason. I feel totally desperate and sad. Lately I have been feeling better, trying to take care of my health and body, trying to go to sleep sooner.

February 6. I feel pretty on top of things, under control, and happy. I had a great practice day, got some bowings done, enjoyed teaching and had two students cancel, nice long chat with my mom, and got to look at some wedding invitation ideas online. I have been looking forward to my two appointments tomorrow for a while: I am meeting with a financial advisor, and I have a wedding dress appointment. I wonder if I'll get to see my dress with real material! I like the idea of being surprised a bit.

March 1. It's the day before my concert. I am prepared, and just finished a yoga class. I just want to make sure I don't over play, and that I stay focused and energized. I was upset when my family called, leaving me messages that they're thinking of coming to the concert and wanting to discuss details ... I'm excited they're coming, I just can't deal with it right now! Tomorrow, I just need every ounce of focus and energy. I will play my very best. I will enjoy the moment. My moment. I am secure. I will be in the moment. I am protected. I am beautiful. I only need to worry about me.

The concert was a spirited delight. My cello and I sang our hearts out. I could sense my colleagues rooting for me and could feel the audience's response. It was a thrill, a rush, a privilege. And afterwards there were flowers.

In addition to my concerto performance, I had agreed to lead my section for the second half of the concert, and my sense of duty was strong. After the exhilaration of finishing my solo, I changed out of my long red dress and back into black concert attire. But a few people asked why I had changed, and after okaying it with both concertmaster and conductor, I changed back into red to lead the section for the rest of the concert.

I was overwhelmed by family members and friends who had traveled to see the performance. We gathered in my parents' hotel room afterwards for sparkling wine and munchies: my parents, grandparents, Graham, my in-laws to be, my godmother, relatives from Boston, friends from Ottawa, and my father, his wife and baby Alex.

We all took turns looking, holding, and admiring Alex, giving him copies of the concert program to play with. I kept up my gracious role, still in my red concert gown, and bounced the baby around. That night, however, I hardly slept, and even though I visited with my family over an early breakfast, it was really hard to leave. I broke down crying in the hallway with my mother. After the biggest performance of my life, instead of giving myself a break, I had planned to rush back to the city to teach, without giving myself a moment to catch my breath. Now, everything had come to a head: the stress and focus of the performance, the intensity of visiting with all of my family in one room. I felt like I had disappeared.

And something else became clear: it was time to end my commute. In June, on the second-last week of the season, I went with my gut feeling and resigned from the orchestra. My exit was graceful and extremely positive. My colleagues were understanding. We played two morning outreach concert services as a string quartet on my last day, and when we were done I packed up in a scramble, as I had a gig in Toronto that night. In my flurry, I accidentally left behind my parting gift and my coat, which contained my keys. I managed to get a ride from the bus station back to the studio to retrieve them before scrambling onto the bus for my last ride back to the city.

Although leaving my job has the natural relief that comes with the end of the season and start of summer, I wonder what September will bring? I will be newly married, with an extra couple of days a week as I will no longer be traveling or doing overnights. Will I start making casseroles? I've heard that's what wives do. Maybe I'll become this Pinterest-worthy domestic queen, and change the colors of our throw pillows for my artistic expression ...

CHAPTER 9

Special, So Special

Our backyard wedding. It's the happiest day in the world. It all comes together as Graham and I take our vows:

I promise to treat you with kindness and respect, and to give you the best of myself, to communicate openly so you can see through the window of my world. To look after myself, so I can be the best partner for you, even when times are challenging. To keep our home filled with love, laughter, music and imagination.

I promise to love you with compassion and gratitude, for the beautiful person you are, my best friend. Completely and forever.

*

Our honeymoon at the family cottage on Lower Beverley Lake was familiar, relaxing and wonderfully inexpensive. Waiting for us upon arrival was a gift from my brother, Pete: charcuterie from the nearby market, a couple of nice wines, and our framed horoscopes cut from *The Globe and Mail* on our wedding day. My parents sent us with a "honeymoon kit" of more wine, chocolate, and bath bombs. My grandmother decked out the double bed with new purple linens, matching reading pillows, and artificial flowers, all ours to take home. Catering leftovers of brisket, pasta salad, baked beans and coleslaw sustained us the first week, and we indulged daily in breakfast pie. I had brought all of the wedding flowers, even the single blooms in tiny cobalt vitamin bottles, so that they could be enjoyed to the last drooping petal. Every time Graham and I changed rooms, my bridal bouquet of roses and succulents joined us in a vase.

We counted turtles from the canoe, savored every wedding card, and took turns winning at Scrabble. The second week, we welcomed my new brother-in-law, for single malt whisky and cards. One evening, as we finished up a game, we were graced by the presence and call of a barred owl. It was all, in short, magical.

Graham and I returned home to our Toronto apartment in late August as happy newlyweds, but I wasted no time getting down to business. Despite being free of my grueling commute, I had apparently learned nothing, and quickly resumed hustling seven days a week: teaching, auditioning for another orchestra, performing with a 25-piece Motown band, and recording with a quartet of opera-pop sopranos. I was high as a kite on all of the possibilities of this new chapter of my life, feeling more awesome than ever.

Since I was on top of everything else, I felt it was finally time to book a doctor's appointment to get to the bottom of my past debilitating depressions. Were my teen depressions "normal" or was there a bigger explanation? The question had lingered for a decade.

I toyed with the possibilities. A cute personality quirk? Moderate general anxiety? Twenty-first century syndrome? No matter what the outcome, I craved closure. When I explained this to my young family doctor, she was completely on board. She was no-nonsense and experienced in mental health. She requisitioned a psychiatric consultation immediately, but warned that it could take months to hear back. I left her office floating on air, feeling damned pleased with myself for being so *thorough*, so *rigorous* in my healthcare. *Look who has her sh*t together!*

A few weeks later, I received a call from the psychiatrist, a woman named Dr. Jeyarajan. I was booked. Now *every* area of my life was under control. I was perfectly on the ball.

I topped off that particular week with a gig as part of a chamber orchestra at a small festival near Ottawa and stayed with one of my bridesmaids, Liz. On the morning of the concert, she and I were enjoying coffee and reminiscing about my wedding when an email from my father came through on my cell phone. It was about Alex, now 18 months old, who had been undergoing tests for a benign bump on his shoulder he'd had since birth.

Dear family and friends, my father wrote. We had it confirmed on Friday that Alexander's illness has progressed to become fibro sarcoma. Our darling little boy has cancer, and in the weeks and months ahead, he will face the battle of his lifetime.

My heart broke. Yet something inside me still believed, still prayed, that Alex would fight this. Modern medicine works miracles. Robust baby boys bounce back, don't they?

One of the pieces of music on the concert program that day was Samuel Barber's "Adagio for Strings." On that glowing early autumn afternoon, the church sanctuary full of patrons, but silent. As the orchestra waited for the conductor's baton, I lifted my bow to the string. The violins ascended, playing one of the most heart-wrenching pieces of music ever written. Visions of a healthy, giggling baby Alexander danced in my mind. I began to weep and held nothing back. With every sonorous note I drew, I drew more tears. This music was for Alex. I released it as my prayer.

Four weeks later the day of my own medical consultation arrived. I was looking forward to the relief it would bring me. In fact, I felt arrogant and cocky as I arrived at the Toronto Western Hospital for my appointment with Dr. Jeyarajan. This would be easy.

I am amazing. Just wait 'til she sees how perfectly I have my sh*t together!

Dr. Jeyarajan was young and beautifully put together, with shiny knee-high black boots. She was approachable, yet her presence commanded authority. I guessed she was still a resident when she told me she would be reviewing my information with her supervisor. I took her seriously.

The assessment began with a detailed personal history that covered my birth to my parents' divorce, through my tumultuous teen depressions, suicide attempt, and a few relapses in my early twenties, all wrapped up with the ribbon of my many accomplishments. Dr. Jeyarajan remained serious. We discussed thoroughly the downs I'd experienced, but I was surprised when she started to ask detailed questions about whether I'd experienced periods of extreme *elevated* mood: elation, specifically paired with lack of sleep and / or any other patterns. "Oh, *absolutely*," I gushed. I had had many of those. Feeling elevated, euphoric and invincible—with flights of creative ideas—was who I *really* was at the core. I had lots to report to Dr. Jeyarajan, and I was actually flattered to be asked! I knew my answers would help refute a diagnosis of depression.

I told her my elevated periods would last anywhere from a week to months at a time. They seemed to precede a period of depression. I would do with little sleep and often find myself incapable of putting down an activity such as a drawing, sewing project or other craft, working incessantly into the night until it was complete. I pointed out that this came in handy for university essays. The same went for practicing my cello in the evenings. I would give my full attention to something and would explode (inside, for the most part) at any disturbance. As for sleep, I described the TV scenes on the insides of my eyelids and the flicking channels in my brain with the looping background music. The price of being creative, you see. I was just so excited, with so many great ideas!

"Would your activity level increase?" she asked. Yes. I would get bursting urges to go running, do a lot of exercise or zoom from task to task. "Did you feel impulsive or hypersexual?"

67

Definitely! I listed my scintillating indiscretions. "Would you present yourself differently during these times, such as in your clothing?" How did she know? Yes, I would typically wear colorful, tighter-fitting clothing and large earrings. At 16, I had shoulder-length dreadlocks and favored a ruffled lime green floor-length sweater. I'd go for bold.

We narrowed down at least two periods when I felt this way: when I was 16, before I had my major depression and suicide attempt, and again at age 18 to 19, when I was in first and second year of university. I reported to Dr. Jeyarajan that during first year I often skipped certain classes, which was out of character, and I failed two courses. I also spent hours of time on boyfriends and extracurricular music productions. I loved being a part of the university music theatre community, playing in the pit for *John and Jen*, *A New Brain*, and *The Last Five Years*, as well as two operas. I adored being the only cellist in a small ensemble, and the music made my heart sing. Not to mention the fun we would have as a band and cast! I would generally feel incredible, and I was very flirtatious. But isn't that what those years are all about?

"Do you like to go on spending sprees? Have you ever spent all of your savings at once?" Dr. Jeyarajan asked. Well, of course. I loved to spend money on things like nice dinners out, and I made impulse purchases all the time, such as the time I won, on eBay, not one but two velvet jingly belly-dance hip-scarves. One fuchsia, one tangerine. They were not cheap. Or that time I splurged on a large tattoo when I turned 18. I was so high on adrenaline that when I was shown the placement of the pressed-on stencil in the mirror, I hastily nodded my approval. It wasn't until the design was made permanent on my raw skin that I realized it was upside-down. Luckily, the simple shapes were symmetrical and easy to touch up and make right. I had expensive tastes all around and I would regularly push the envelope on my finances, but my spending would definitely increase when I was feeling euphoric. At that time I worked weekend shifts at a local pub and taught a couple of students, so I was used to having some disposable income.

Dr. Jeyarajan continued, unwavering. "Did you experience feelings of grandiosity? As if you had special powers, or believed you were God?"

"Oh absolutely," I blurted. When I'm feeling amazing, I generally think I am a superior human, with extra-special abilities. Magical, even. Sometimes I think I am psychic, that I see "signs" everywhere. I sometimes believe that I am secretly an award-winning novelist, but I just haven't written the book yet.

I was nailing this interview.

The consultation was supposed to take 45 to 60 minutes, but Dr. Jeyarajan worked with me for over two hours. She was being thorough. She also had to take into account how special I was. Even better, after relating so many wonderfully positive experiences, there was *no way* I had depression. I was sure that she would find me to be either completely normal, or diagnose me with a very common, boring affliction, like mild social anxiety. On my way out I booked my follow-up appointment. Now all there was to do was wait.

Five hours later, I was onstage at The Flying Beaver Pubaret in the gay village with my black carbon fiber cello and matching eyeliner, grooving to a packed house with Elton-John-meets-Rufus-Wainwright original pop tunes. We soaked up applause and completed a perfect evening with plenty of schmoozing, martinis and beer.

October 28 was the day of my follow-up psychiatric appointment. It started like any other day. I taught in the morning before rushing out to what I expected to be an ordinary meeting. I was greeted at 3:00 pm by Dr. Jeyarajan's tall and kindly supervisor, Dr. Parikh, who sported a dark goatee, glasses, and a cheesy cartoon tie. Shaking his hand and smiling, I confidently strolled in and plopped on the leather couch. Facing both psychiatrists, I smiled and tossed my long highlights, like a child expecting a reward. I felt assured that I was as balanced as could be.

The doctors asked if I had any more questions or anything else I wanted to share. I came prepared with notes, and filled them in with the rest of my family history. There was some family history of depression, anxiety, alcoholism and other issues on both parents' sides, including trauma and agoraphobia. I also relayed incidents that I had dissociated from and forgotten to share earlier: my sexual assault at age nine and the severe bullying that followed, as well as assaults on other occasions. I wasn't sure if it was relevant. The doctors nodded quietly, before dropping the bomb that would change my life forever.

Dr. Jeyarajan spoke. "It looks very likely that you have bipolar disorder."

I was struck dumb for a moment, and then I didn't know where to start. "What? Really? Are you sure?" I didn't understand what bipolar disorder really was, but I knew it was something bad. I was in instant denial.

Dr. Parikh's voice was deep and steady: "We are about 90–95% certain."

"There were a few other experiences of elevated mood that I forgot to mention!" I blurted, thinking this was about depression, thinking it would save me.

"Okay. Then we are about 95–97% certain."

Wait, *what*? My mind raced with images, caricatures of what I thought bipolar disorder looked like: the swaggering "crazy" man on our street who was always shouting. Pierced and mohawked teens squabbling over smokes and begging for change. The unkempt homeless woman twitching and muttering to herself. Monstrous humans with terrible tempers fluctuating between hot and cold throughout the day. I thought of the tempers that ran in my family. I really had no idea. I was a successful, accomplished young woman with graduate school education. My temperament was nowhere close to being an on / off switch: people praised me for always being so positive, so *delightful*. I had my sh*t together!

The doctors appeared to disagree with my self-assessment. Soberly, they explained that at least one of my elevated mood experiences was actually a manic episode.

Manic episode?! I thought my elevated moods were my ticket to Sane Town! What could be problematic about feeling amazing? I came here to check out my *depressions*. Wasn't that what this was all supposed to be about?

Dr. Parikh explained that according to the DSM, it takes one—one—manic episode to earn a diagnosis of bipolar disorder. Someone can experience a manic episode and not have another for months or many years.

Rather than explain the details of the illness to me right then and there, Dr. Parikh handed me a printout of suggested books and resources to check out, which would help answer my questions. He assured me that I would have thousands of questions. While he explained that medication is an essential route of treatment, both doctors acknowledged that I would need some time to think it through. My immediate thought was to not take any medication, and I made that very clear. Whatever this thing meant, I would *not* be taking any drugs. "Can't I just sniff some lavender, keep up my yoga and take more bubble baths?" I asked. No one told me no, but we decided to make a follow-up appointment after I'd had some time to process things.

Dr. Parikh then surprised me with a tremendous gesture: he asked me to take some time to decide if I thought the diagnosis was the right fit. I was given the choice whether or not to accept it, and could decide for myself if it resonated with me. They didn't label me; they didn't "do" this to me. The choice was mine.

Looking back, this was an incredibly progressive, empowering offering by a medical professional. I now know that not everyone who seeks treatment is handed such a lucky card. But at the time, as I left the office in a daze, I found myself becoming very angry. *Who is this bozo, Parikh? I'll bet he doesn't know what the hell he is talking about. He's probably some label-happy generalist. What the hell does he know?* I pulled my smartphone out of my knitted rainbow-colored pouch and Googled him in the hallway.

He was not only the Deputy Psychiatrist-in-Chief at the hospital, Director of Continuing Mental Health Education at the University of Toronto, and Head of General

Psychiatry, but he was previously head of the Bipolar Clinic at the Centre for Addiction and

Mental Health. He co-authored CANMAT's (Canadian Network for Mood and Anxiety Treatments) treatment guidelines for depression and bipolar disorder. And he had earned one international, two national and three local awards for teaching.

Oh.

CHAPTER 10

Exclusive Club Membership

I went home and told Graham my news. Like me, he reacted with a combination of denial and dismissal, compartmentalizing it to process later. Out of desperation, my next instinct was to call my mom. Looking back, I realize it was a mistake, as I didn't know enough (read: *anything*) about bipolar disorder to be able to calmly and accurately explain the illness and prognosis, or adequately prepare her for the bomb I was about to drop. But I was frightened. I needed my mom.

She must have been home early or taken a lieu day from work, because she was conditioning her hair with henna at home. I could picture her puttering around the house or relaxing on the couch, her head wrapped in mud and plastic. Without thinking—not taking any of her cues, not saving this conversation for when I knew more and could choose my time—I asked if it was a good time to talk. I didn't realize the severity of what I was telling her, and didn't give her a moment to prepare what to say. I couldn't wait. I needed her now. She sounded rushed and distracted, but exclaimed, "Sure!"

My voice wavered as I told her that after years of wondering, I thought I finally had an answer about my mental health.

I was searching my limited store of knowledge to explain what bipolar disorder really was when she burst out, "But what about *Graham*?! He just married you!" Graham overheard this part of the conversation and poked his head out of our bedroom doorway with a grin and a thumbs-up. "But you are so *stable*!" she exclaimed. "This is a huge surprise. *Huge*!" Exactly. I thought I was stable, save for some normal troubled teen moments. My whole life I had been told I was perfectly normal and in perfect health. A superlative human being.

The rest of the week, I somehow managed to carry on with my teaching, have some friends over, submit a grant application for a Baroque program, and rehearse for an orchestral gig, all the while wondering, grieving, researching, Googling, and scrolling Wikipedia repeatedly for any and every piece of information regarding bipolar disorder. So many thoughts raced through my head. *Can people tell that I'm crazy? Will my aunt and uncle detect it when I babysit their kid next week?* I felt like I was hiding a huge secret that might leak out and ruin me. My diagnosis was so fresh, so confusing. It felt like a violation. I had to repeatedly check with Graham that it was all really happening. Sometimes I just wept.

But being a woman of action, I promptly attacked Dr. Parikh's suggested reading and resource sheet. I learned that it is the presence of mania that defines bipolar disorder. Because it is so difficult to diagnose (as manic symptoms feel so fantastic, the patient doesn't report them as problematic), sufferers can go years—even decades—without a proper diagnosis. As luck would have it, I was actually in a manic phase when I decided to investigate my mental health once and for all. In other words, my illness drove me to investigate and uncover my illness.

Slowly, albeit with some internal resistance, the puzzle pieces began to fit together, especially when I learned that bipolar disorder is often misdiagnosed as depression and that symptoms usually begin in the teens or early twenties. I quickly became acquainted with the different types and subtypes of bipolar disorder. Because I had had at least one full manic episode, according to Dr. Parikh, it "earned me a ticket" to the bipolar I club.

While I was still raw and wrestling with my diagnosis, I received other troubling news.

Dear family and friends, my father wrote. Alexander's chemotherapy has failed to save him. His cancer has spread to his lung. His chemotherapy has been stopped and he is now in the care of the palliative team. We welcome you to come to our home to visit him and get to know a little better this wonderful, bright, jolly little boy, who has enriched us beyond measure. The pain in our hearts is unbearable, the aggressiveness and evil of this disease incomprehensible.

My brother Pete came over to talk about Alex and to discuss plans for us to make multiple trips to Ottawa over the following weeks. I decided, without hesitation, to also share my diagnosis with him. I think I caught him off guard, too. He was taken aback and didn't seem to know what to say, but I wasn't going to hide it from my brother, especially since bipolar disorder runs in families. To cope with Alex, we needed each other. To cope with my illness, I needed my brother, too.

In early November, I went to my first drop-in support group at the Mood Disorders Association of Ontario. I was shocked to discover how much I belonged, and the experience comforted me. I realized that between my grief about our little brother and being diagnosed with a mental illness, I needed to reach out and share with someone else—anyone else. I would need support to carry what seemed like a secret boulder.

I also decided to email a singer I had worked with in a performance long ago. I remembered that she had mentioned in passing, during a rehearsal, that she was bipolar. I didn't think anything of it at the time, but now that we were in the same boat, I thought I'd try to connect:

Hi,

I noticed you are back after a Facebook hiatus—what a great idea!

I am writing to you—I could have this completely wrong—because I remember a long time ago at a rehearsal, you mentioned having bipolar disorder.

If I remembered wrong, please disregard all of this and consider this a "Hey!" Well, I was diagnosed with bipolar disorder a week ago, which came as a very big surprise. Now that I am getting to know more about it, it is starting to make more sense to me ...

I wanted to write you, in case my memory was correct, because I am in partial denial and in search of peer support, and would love to talk about it sometime over coffee. I joined a bipolar drop-in peer support group at the Mood Disorders Association of Ontario and went yesterday. It was very eye-opening, and it scared me a little that I felt at home. I hope you are keeping really well, and that maybe my memory was right. I'm sure it goes without saying that I'm keeping my news confidential at the moment :)

Hope we cross paths soon,

Erika (cello!)

I received a wonderful reply.

Hi there!!

You remember correctly! I would be more than happy to get together and chat. I can certainly say I know how you feel. I'm really proud of you for reaching out right away and checking out support groups. It's frightening and awkward, but you will be better off in the long run. In fact, I would love to talk to you about your experience at the support group. That's something I've been frightened to do but have been thinking about it a lot. I can tell you that the people at the Mood Disorders Association are amazing.

I shall definitely keep this to myself, I totally understand. Let me know your schedule, I work 9–5 in the west end but can meet you in the evenings.

Also feel free to call or text.

Wishing you much love!!

The next morning I had another appointment with Dr. Parikh. I was trying to keep up my weekly routines and be "normal," but I was starting to feel depressed, like I was slipping away. I was confused as to whether this was a normal response to grief or if I was sinking into a depressive episode. By then, I knew that for people with bipolar disorder, episodes can be triggered by stress. With the double-barreled shock of being diagnosed with a mental illness and hearing that my baby brother had terminal cancer, I had plenty of stress. I was still considering taking medication; I thought it might be a good idea, but not just yet, which is what I told Dr. Parikh. He didn't pressure me, but he did explain how lithium works and how it can shorten the life of a depressive episode before it escalates. He said it also has an excellent profile of preventing suicide.

The following day I had breakfast with my good friend Livia. I waited until near the end to tell her both pieces of bad news. I just wanted to have a normal, chatty date with my friend. She couldn't believe that I had held my news in that long. She cried when I told her about Alex; as a mother, she knew that what had happened was the unthinkable. Regarding my bipolar diagnosis, she encouraged me to at least get a second opinion, on the grounds that doctors misdiagnose all the time. She went on to tell a story of a friend who poured endless time and years of energy into an illness that turned out to be a complete mistake. If I was going to spend energy on this, I'd want to be really sure. She was right.

As we walked to the car, Livia put her arm around me. "I don't do small talk," she said. "I know I'm busy with the baby and work, but I want to know what's going on. Really. In your life." I went home with tears of joy that I could have such a true friend.

Later that day, I saw my family doctor and asked for more testing for a second opinion. She was right on the ball and sent for another opinion right away. I also told her that I wanted to go off my birth control and return to a "blank slate." If I was going to take psychiatric medication, I didn't want any other drug interfering with my hormones and moods.

My second opinion appointment was as revealing as my initial assessment. After describing all of my symptoms to a third psychiatrist, he told me that I had basically described the illness to him. A textbook case.

But I *was* getting depressed. I couldn't stop crying, I couldn't get dressed or shower, and for the first time ever, I canceled student lessons. My thoughts turned to walking into traffic. My husband, the rock that he is, made a deal with me: I was going to go shower and we would walk together to the subway station down the street, just to get out of the house and do *something*. It was a small step that felt like an enormous task. So, despite my prejudice against medication, my fear of being flattened, my reluctance to admit I was "broken," and my deep-seated fear of losing my creativity and my music, I accepted the idea of starting to take something before my situation got worse. On Friday, November 29, I allowed Dr. Parikh to write me a prescription for lithium, to be filled whenever I was ready.

I was ready. That afternoon I came home with my bottle of cute little pink pills. Starting now, I would begin a new life.

PART II

CHAPTER 1

Walking, I Make the Road

THAT WAS THEN, THIS IS NOW

When I was diagnosed with bipolar disorder at the age of 27, I faced a complete life overhaul. And when I finally accepted the diagnosis and agreed to take medication, I sensed that a new life was beginning for me. Even so, the prospect of change—so much, so soon, so profound—overwhelmed me. There were no precedents for me to follow. I didn't know where to begin. I didn't know whether living well with a mental illness was possible. I couldn't imagine how to go about changing. Changing what, exactly?

So, I did the only thing I could do: I simply set out on the journey. At first my steps were tiny, shaky ones, and I wasn't always sure where to put my feet. But as the poem by Antonio Machado[3] suggests, it was only by walking that I made the road. With time I became more sure-footed and more familiar with the signposts, more accepting of help from passers-by and fellow travelers, and more rewarded for my efforts. I began practicing self-care on a macro scale: I changed how I approached my daily routine and my work schedule. I modified how I ate and looked after myself. I altered my lifestyle and my attitudes about money. I replaced old beliefs with new ones, many of them counter-cultural, like where technology fits in my life or what it means to be creative and productive. The result was a holistic plan that touches every aspect of my life and works for me.

The concept of living well looks different from person to person, and each of us must define it for ourselves. When I tried living someone else's idea of living well I became ill, and found myself on a new path where I had to redefine living well in the context of living with a mental illness. For me, living well means that I function effectively and smoothly in the activities I do. I feel rested, energized, calm, steady, and relaxed, which allows me to share my best self with others and the people I love most. Above all, living well does not mean living perfectly; rather, it is about living in balance, living authentically, and living my truth.

While I sometimes still stumble and fall, and wonder if I will ever get up again, my new path leads the way, and I keep walking. I am now healthier, happier, and more fulfilled than I've ever been before.

What follows is what I learned about bipolar disorder after my diagnosis, and the plan that I developed for living well, and eventually thriving with bipolar disorder. The general information that I provide is not medical advice; it is what I, as a person with a diagnosed mood disorder, have learned through my own research and education in order to understand my medical situation. For any of the mental health conditions explored in this book, consult your doctor or psychiatrist to discuss your specific symptoms and get answers to any questions you may have.

BIPOLAR BASICS

When I started learning about bipolar disorder, I was shocked at how different the illness was compared to what I erroneously *thought* it was. I was completely ignorant, and without knowing it, harbored stigmas of my own. The way I pictured it was way off, like a monstrous caricature. I have since researched bipolar disorder extensively to learn about my condition, and what follows is an introduction to what bipolar disorder *really* looks like.

The term "bipolar disorder" refers to gradual, yet extreme mood swings that occur between two poles: high and low; mania and depression. It was originally called "manic depressive illness." In contrast, in the case of major depression, mood swings only fall to one pole—the lows—which is why it is sometimes referred to as "unipolar disorder." It is important to note that between high and low episodes, a person can feel well and function well.

With bipolar disorder, episodes of either mania or depression can last anywhere from days to months. Learning about the length of mood episodes surprised me, even though I experienced those exact symptoms. I had always pictured bipolar mood swings as occurring rapidly, imagining them cycling up and down, hot and cold throughout the day. Now I know that that is not what happens, although some can experience a greater frequency called "rapid cycling."

Symptoms of depressive episodes often present themselves first in the life of someone with bipolar disorder, usually in the teens or early twenties. Because of this, bipolar disorder is often misdiagnosed as major depression in the beginning, resulting in the patient being prescribed unsuitable medications. Depressive episodes are characterized by feelings that go beyond sadness or feeling "down in the dumps." A person suffering from depression loses interest in things they once enjoyed, experiences a loss or increase of appetite, feels chronically fatigued, has difficulty sleeping (either too little or too much), generally feels guilty and badly about themself, has trouble making decisions and concentrating, and may have recurring thoughts of suicide.

When a manic episode eventually occurs—usually following the initial depressive episode—it is commonly not investigated, even when it yields destructive behavior. The symptoms masquerade as extremely positive and pleasurable feelings, just like they did for me. During manic episodes, people are unable to see that anything is wrong; in fact, they often become so grandiose that they think they are *awesome* and feeling better than ever. On the other hand, sometimes bipolar does get investigated during a manic episode simply because that is when a person with bipolar disorder is most likely to contact a medical professional. During depressive episodes, people with bipolar disorder are more likely to withdraw from interaction and often don't have the capacity to seek help.

Unlike depression, mania and hypomania (a less extreme mania) are not widely familiar to people, and as a result they are commonly misunderstood. Mania and hypomania tend to elicit an excessively happy or expansive mood (known as "euphoric mania"). When experiencing euphoric mania, people present as elated. They are productive, tend to speak rapidly, and have racing flights of ideas. They have a marked decreased need for sleep, despite their increased energy and activity levels. They often have an inflated sense of self-esteem and of their own abilities. They can also present negatively (known as "dysphoric mania") and experience an excessively irritable, touchy, and angry mood, along with changes in thinking and perception. Reckless, impulsive behavior can be present in both types of mania.

A percentage of those with bipolar disorder experience frightening "mixed episodes," where both mania and depression are experienced simultaneously.

Episodes of mania and depression vary greatly and can present themselves differently from person to person. It is also important to note that episodes and symptoms of bipolar disorder do not develop overnight. Do not try to diagnose yourself or others on your own. If you suspect any symptoms, discuss them with a healthcare provider.

RECOGNIZING SIGNS THAT YOU ARE UNWELL: GETTING THE RIGHT DIAGNOSIS

One of the most important steps to getting help with a mental illness is getting an accurate diagnosis. Once I had the correct diagnosis in place, I was able to begin a targeted treatment plan.

Many mental illnesses are misdiagnosed at first. As I mentioned before, bipolar disorder often presents as major depression in the early stages of the illness. It often only becomes recognized as bipolar disorder when SSRI's, a class of drugs commonly prescribed as antidepressants, don't work for the patient, or the patient experiences a manic episode.

While it is important for people with bipolar disorder to pay attention to the major symptoms they have been having, there are also lesser-known symptoms to consider that could indicate that they should check in with their healthcare provider. It is especially important to pay attention to multiple symptoms that occur over multiple days.

Symptoms of a Depressive Episode

The symptoms of depression in bipolar disorder include at least five of the following[4], and are present for most days, all day, and for at least two weeks:

- A sad, despairing mood that impairs your performance at school, work or in social situations
- Agitation or apathy
- Changes in appetite
- Feeling useless, hopeless, worthless, or excessively guilty; or experiencing low self-esteem
- Insomnia or hypersomnia (not sleeping or oversleeping)
- Loss of energy
- Loss of interest in school, work, hobbies or intimacy
- Marked loss of interest or pleasure in activities that used to be enjoyable
- Thoughts of suicide (which must *always* be taken seriously)
- Weight changes, loss or gain
- Withdrawal from family members or friends

Most people can recognize the above symptoms of depression, but there are many other symptoms that might not be as obvious[5]:

- Difficulty concentrating
- Difficulty making decisions
- Difficulty remembering, or challenges with memory
- Irritability
- Overall fatigue
- Problems falling asleep or staying asleep

Symptoms of a Manic Episode

A manic episode is, in short, an unusually highly elevated mood. A person experiencing a manic episode can appear abnormally and continuously high, happy, and expansive (euphoric) or they may present as irritable, angry, and aggressive (dysphoric). The symptoms of hypomania are less severe than those of mania. A person experiencing hypomania may feel happy and have a lot of energy, but their behavior does not seriously disrupt their life[6]. Hypomania, however, can progress to full-blown mania, or to a depressive episode, and therefore still requires treatment. In a manic phase of bipolar disorder, a person with the more common type II bipolar disorder may experience hypomania, while a person with type I may experience a full-blown manic episode. A manic episode includes at least three of the following symptoms, and persists over a week or more:

- A decreased need for sleep
- An increase in talking
- Delusional thinking
- Exaggerated self-esteem or feeling grandiose
- Flights of ideas or racing thoughts
- Impulsivity, especially with spending habits or sex
- Irritability
- Losing touch with reality
- Poor judgement
- Psychotic symptoms
- Seeing or hearing things
- Sped-up activities

Symptoms of a Psychotic Episode

When episodes of mania or depression escalate, the person suffering can begin experiencing symptoms of psychosis, which is the term used to describe a condition where a person has a difficult time distinguishing between what is real and what is not. A first episode of psychosis can be particularly frightening because the experience is unfamiliar. Psychosis usually appears for the first time in a person's teens or late twenties. The experience of psychosis varies from person to person, and it can develop gradually or come on suddenly. Symptoms of psychosis include[8]:

- Cognitive symptoms, such as difficulties with memory and concentration
- Delusions
- Difficulty generating thoughts or ideas
- Disorganized speech, thoughts, or behavior
- Hallucinations, such as seeing, hearing, tasting or smelling something that is not actually there
- Mood changes
- Reduced ability to begin tasks
- Reduced motivation and socialization
- Sleep disturbances
- Suicidal thoughts or behaviors

The Subtypes of Bipolar Disorder

According to the codes published by the American Psychiatric Association (the *Diagnostic and Statistical Manual of Mental Disorders, Fifth Edition*[9]) and used by mental health professionals to describe the features of a mental health disorder, bipolar disorder can be subdivided into the following categories. Competent healthcare providers will have an understanding of each of these subtypes.

Bipolar I disorder:

- At least one lifetime episode of manic or mixed disorder

- Although not required for the diagnosis, at least one lifetime episode of major depressive disorder

Bipolar II disorder:
- At least one lifetime episode of hypomanic disorder
- At least one lifetime episode of major depressive disorder

Bipolar disorder not otherwise specified (NOS):
- Multiple manic episodes with impairment of functioning that do not meet the DSM-IV-TR duration criteria or that fall one symptom short of the required number of symptoms

Bipolar disorder with rapid cycling:
- Meets criteria for bipolar I or bipolar II disorder
- Four or more episodes of major depressive disorder, manic disorder, mixed disorder, or hypomanic disorder in any one year

Although it was a shock to receive a diagnosis of bipolar disorder and learn that I had the more severe type I, this knowledge helped me understand my illness and move forward in learning how to treat my unique symptoms. I have provided the above information for context and background, but please note that it is not a replacement for a medical diagnosis provided by a professional healthcare provider. A diagnosis is an essential first step in treating any mental illness.

CHAPTER 2

finding the Right Medication

For many, living with bipolar disorder means taking medication daily and, sometimes, begrudging that fact. It is okay to periodically resent your medication, as I did, and wish you didn't have to take it. At first, I felt it was a daily reminder that I was unwell or "broken," but I've since come to realize that medication is an essential element in the treatment of this condition. It doesn't mean I'm "broken" or defective in any way. Now a regular feature of my life, medication is something that I value and accept. I treat my illness first. I've found that many social aspects and some symptoms are better managed in other ways, such as through psychotherapy, but medication for bipolar disorder is a necessary component of my holistic health plan.

I CHOOSE MY MEDICATION

When I was diagnosed with bipolar disorder and before I understood the severity of my illness, I flatly rejected medication without a second thought. Surely there was a supplement, I reasoned, or an environmental change I could make instead of medication? Couldn't I just try to relax more?

A heavy stigma surrounds mental illness, but an equally weighty one surrounds medication. I resisted medication because this stigma was deeply ingrained in me from as far back as high school, when I was prescribed Prozac after my family doctor diagnosed me with depression. Society and my upbringing told me that taking medication was shameful and meant that something was seriously wrong with me. "Drugs" weren't natural.

It took time, but I finally came to understand that taking medication is a pillar in the successful treatment of *many* illnesses, including mental illnesses. My first psychiatrist helped put this in perspective by comparing medication to nutrition. When you are deficient in a nutrient, he explained, you obtain that nutrient by consuming more foods that contain it, or perhaps by adding a supplement. When you have a mental health condition like bipolar disorder, your brain is deficient in essential chemical reactions and neural cellular connectivity, and taking medication is what treats this deficiency. So now my attitude is that if someone with type 1 diabetes needs to combat an insulin deficiency with routine insulin injections—or someone with iron deficiency anemia needs to supplement their iron intake regularly—then it makes sense for me to take daily medication for my brain. And when I began taking lithium to treat my bipolar disorder, knowing that lithium was a natural element like iron made me feel better about "being on meds." It also helped that my pills were tiny and pink. Hey, whatever works!

I also use a technique called "reframing" to ease the feelings of obligation and resentment that I sometimes feel toward my disorder. Whenever I catch myself saying "I *have* to," I replace it with "I *choose* to[10]." When I reframe I look at an obligation from a constructive yet realistic vantage point, one that acknowledges responsibility rather than focusing on the negative (that only leaves me feeling trapped and victimized). For example, instead of saying "I have to take my medicine," I try to use a more positive phrase: "I *choose* to take my medicine, so I can stay well and live my best life." Marshall B. Rosenberg, PhD, describes this as "replacing language that implies a lack of choice with language that acknowledges choice." This technique can work for many aspects of life: "I *have* to work" becomes "I *choose* to work, because it helps me pay my bills and live comfortably. It allows me to share music—an art form that is deeply meaningful to me—with others."

Finding a combination of medications that is effective in treating bipolar disorder can sometimes take years of trial and error. Even if you find a medication that is effective, it may have side effects that are difficult to live with. Some side effects are easy to manage, while others are not.

It took me nearly two years to find the right combination of medications that controlled my symptoms, prevented further episodes, and had side effects that I could handle. For example, one medication I took caused me to experience cognitive delay and difficulty with speech, and this made my work and personal life too challenging. When I switched to other medications these side effects went away, but were replaced by others. My current medication causes me to sleep upwards of 10 hours a night. I work around this by making sure that I take my medication at the same time each evening—10 hours before my alarm goes off in the morning. I am comfortable managing this tradeoff while we wait for new drugs to emerge that have no side effects at all.

Cost is another important consideration. Some medications are prohibitively expensive, depending on factors including the country you live in. When my spouse's drug coverage ended and we had to pay for my medication out of pocket, I did the math: one of my medications would cost me $5 *per pill*. Some medications cost even more than this.

However, I was fortunate to learn of a trick that drastically cuts my costs. Where I live, the cost of one of my medications is *per pill*, as opposed to *per dose*. So, my psychiatrist agreed to write me a prescription for pills that are twice my daily dose of medication—40 mg instead of 20 mg—and I now cut my tablets in half with a pill splitter, literally cutting the cost in half. Check with your doctor first, as many medications have a special coating and might not be designed to be split.

Reaching a state of acceptance about my bipolar disorder has taken time and effort, but it has all been worthwhile. I now value and protect my medication immensely, especially when I consider how I would be functioning without it. That thought still frightens me, so I make sure to have extra doses with me at all times, just in case.

Some people need to take supplements for nutrient deficiencies. Some need anti-inflammatory drugs for pain. Some need antibiotics for infections. Some take a statin because they have an elevated risk of cardiovascular disease. And, some, like me, need to take medication for chemical imbalances in their brain. We need to recognize that bipolar disorder and other mental illnesses are just illnesses like any other.

THE DRUGS DO WORK

I was astonished when I made a list of the benefits of my medication. In addition to treating the major symptoms of bipolar disorder, my medication resolved many subtle day-to-day symptoms that used to add up to a whole lot of stress! I can't believe that I used to cope with all of these challenges on a daily basis. Behold, my list:

- **I'm no longer easily provoked to extreme irritation.**

I can now tolerate, and even ignore, things that used to make me feel like exploding several times a day and lead me to lose all concentration: an itch caused by an inner tag on my clothing; loud gum chewing; sniffing or coughing ("body sounds"); a ringing phone; the roar of a vacuum cleaner; clanging dishes or other sudden noises; any quiet, repetitive sounds like a dripping faucet; the chatter of a baseball game on TV; not getting my way; coworkers interrupting me; my spouse puttering in another room while I'm trying to work; the distant sound of a tinkering jazz pianist ... and other human beings in general! I realize now that feeling irritated nearly all the time exhausted me. To avoid alienating or offending other people, I had to constantly hold in my irritation and suppress the urge to react angrily. Such outbursts—extreme and puzzling to others and even to me—had happened on many occasions in the past, with friends, family, and coworkers bearing the brunt. Behaviors that I used to attribute to "low blood sugar" or "being tired" were actually symptoms of bipolar disorder that were simply magnified by being hungry or tired.

- **I can now enjoy thinking about only one thing at a time.**

My previous preoccupation with *every little detail* was completely overwhelming. A scattered collection of thoughts would swirl in my mind 24 / 7. This was exhausting and made it hard to concentrate. My mind was like an overflowing jar of gourmet jelly beans in every flavor. Now, the jar is two-thirds full, and only contains the best flavors. When I first experienced how medication could help slow down and separate my thoughts, I couldn't believe that I had spent *years* functioning the other way.

- **I can see things realistically.**

To experience extreme emotion naturally leads to extreme descriptions. I used to blather on emphatically and passionately about an item or event, and I wasn't shy to exaggerate. I am still passionate and excited about my favorite things and I have dislikes—I'm just now able to talk about them in a way that is proportionate.

- **I can take a hit.**

I used to be oversensitive to jokes and criticisms, which would trigger rumination, overthinking, and paranoia. My medication helps with the anxiety and rumination, and my growing insight through therapy has helped me understand that criticism often says more about the other person than it does about you. I love being able to laugh at myself now, and I no longer take things personally.

- **I am able to sleep deeply and without interruption.**

Before taking medication, I wasn't actually sleeping. I just thought I was. And since I wasn't really sleeping, waking up in the morning was rough, almost physically painful. I interpreted this as a moral failure on my part: I felt lazy for not popping out of bed at

6:00 am like my parents. By the afternoon I would be exhausted, zoning out, and desperate for a nap. But somehow, come evening, my energy would return, and I would stay up extremely late. While lying awake in bed, I would entertain myself by "watching" my racing thoughts and listening to the accompanying background music. I didn't feel tired in the slightest and interpreted these vivid "visions" as dream-filled sleep. Nope. Now, because of the sedating qualities of one of my medications, I enjoy up to 10 hours of true, deep, uninterrupted sleep each night. And I feel rested and alert in all my waking hours, without the urge to nap. (I like to joke that I take a daily nap between 7:00 am and 8:30 am!)

- **I saved my teeth.**

While I still sleep with a night guard, I no longer clench my jaw and grind my teeth at night (my dentist is happy about that!).

- **I wake up to quiet.**

In the years leading up to my diagnosis, as far back as I can remember, I would wake up in the morning hearing music, usually children's songs, which turned out to be auditory hallucinations. While it was fun listening to the "song of the day" on my inner jukebox, I relish the quiet I now have, and I can start my day afresh without being lulled into listening to a concert in bed.

- **I can listen.**

I now ask others how their day is going and can really, truly listen and hear their responses. I rarely "tune out" when others are speaking anymore. If I start to lose my ability to listen and stay present, I recognize that as a sign that I am becoming unwell.

- **I can think clearly and operate in an organized, systematic manner.**

Since my medicine has helped slow down my racing thoughts, I am able to concentrate and easily remember little details, such as what I need to pack in my gig bag for a rehearsal or that I need to reply to an email. There is no longer scrambling, chaos, and "last-minute panic" while I am running out the door; I prepare the night before for the next day. I still rush sometimes, but without shaking from stress, forgetting essential items, or experiencing pit-of-my-stomach panic, confusion and disorientation.

- **I can better handle a full day.**

The occasional really busy day no longer leaves me physically and emotionally wrecked, feeling buzzed, overwhelmed, and frazzled, with shallow breathing and tightness in my chest.

- **I am *far* less flighty.**

I used to be "famous" in my family for being "ditzy" and forgetting important information or items. In middle school I was nicknamed "Phoebe" after the free-spirited blonde musician from the American sitcom *Friends*. Not anymore. Now, I'm known for being organized and on the ball.

- **I can better handle my city.**

I am able to live in a busy city, without the desperate need for respite every few weeks. I used to feel constantly anxious and crave time in the country or at a cottage. I still need to escape—urban life can be taxing—but now I can handle months of city living at a time.

I think of my years before treating my bipolar disorder and taking medication as "swimming upstream." Day-to-day activities were challenging for me, and I was working extra hard to overcome hundreds of obstacles all day, every day, without even realizing it. When I accepted my need to take medication and found a combination of meds that was right for me, I was rewarded with a "new normal"—a pleasant, daily solidity that allows me to look back on past experiences through a lens of understanding.

MANIA: NOT THE SAME AS CREATIVITY

Since I have type I bipolar disorder, I am more prone to manic episodes than to depression. Manic episodes are bouts of frenzied, elated energy that last for days. They start out as hypomania, which is less severe and presents as an enjoyable, fun and sociable elevated state. In those with type I, hypomania can escalate into a full-blown mania, which can include delusions and psychosis. People who have the more common type II bipolar disorder occasionally experience bouts of hypomania, but are more prone to depression.

I used to equate my mania with my creativity, and I mourned the loss of what I thought was my best creative self to medication, thinking I would never get it back. I was wrong. Now, when I compare being stable on medication (what I used to think of as "boring") to the whirlwind of fabulousness that I experienced in a manic state (what I used to think of as "fun"), I know which one I prefer. And even though I am generally stable while taking my medication, I have had several manic symptom breakthroughs and found that they no longer have the same allure they once did. Breakthroughs occur when the conditions are just right and a number of factors are present; for me, these usually include poor sleep from late gigs followed by early mornings, too many busy days in a row, a change of routine, or too much overall excitement.

When I am experiencing a hypomanic episode, I have flights of ideas and racing thoughts. I morph into a chatterbox with boundless (sometimes hypersexual) energy. I jump from one task or idea to another without completing anything, or become obsessive about a specific project, idea or item. Recent incidents include listening to Brian Wilson's record "Love and Mercy" more than eight times in a row (because I thought it was *amazing*) while repotting all of our houseplants, or when I became obsessed with the idea of selling multiple possessions to acquire a $135 Depression-era green glass citrus reamer to make whiskey sours. Though these experiences may seem quirky, pleasant and benign, others are not. I sometimes spew venom and am extremely impatient, snappy, and irritable with those who can't keep up or dare try to stop or interrupt me. I have grandiose thoughts, consider myself a genius, and basically operate at warp speed, while everything around me seems to sparkle with glitter and unicorns. If the hypomania escalates to mania, I experience delusions and psychosis that lead me to hear voices and believe that I have magical powers, such as the ability to communicate with gods or spirits (that I don't actually believe in). That's when my mania gets scarier.

One summer, during an exciting week of activities away from home, I found myself in the shower, obsessed with fitting my head and body into the smooth, concave shape of the inner corners of the stall. I wanted to phone everyone I knew to tell them about this incredible discovery. With my hands outstretched to the ceiling in prayer under the flowing warm water, I conjured gods to thank them for giving me such magical abilities. I went on to thank them for giving me the gift of being able to experience all five of my senses so intensely, as well as the true beauty of art, music, nature, and the world. I felt a sensation of orgasmic glitter coming out of my skin. It was magical. I was magical. The scary part is that I was having a psychotic hallucination. In retrospect, this was not a proud moment, but while I am in this state, my symptoms make up a very seductive package.

You see, when I am having manic symptoms, I *feel* more creative, my ideas *feel* abundant, and I *feel* like my most amazing self. But that isn't really the case. My spouse has commented that although he has enjoyed spending time with me when I was "high"—and he knew me this way for many years before my diagnosis—he prefers spending time with me when I am as stable as I am now. This was a major reality check! Together we have also analyzed my symptoms, compared them to when I am stable, and made some interesting observations. For example, while I *feel* more creative when manic, in reality my racing thoughts are not coherent, and I cannot articulate them well. I cannot complete the tasks I start, and I do not accomplish more. With few exceptions, I am not a better version of myself. *It just feels that way.*

At first, my elevated state appears to be productive, but it has a limit; as my energy escalates it becomes counterproductive.

As a girl I would stay up late, relentlessly working on a sewing or art project, without even pausing to use the restroom. As I worked furiously into the night, I would start making mistakes—big ones—that left me ripping apart beautiful fabric or machine-stitching wrong parts together. And as a teen, there were writing projects that felt like brilliant, poetic free falls, which would later read as incoherent, chaotic messes.

When I was first preparing my book proposal, the excitement of getting a draft to my editor as quickly as possible had me slip into a former state, typing frantically enough to forget my appetite, put off visiting the restroom, and let the kettle boil dry on the gas stove. The only difference was that I managed to keep my work to daytime hours. In the final stages of creating this book, I squeezed editing between cello students, calls to the UK, performing an all Cheap Trick concert, and rehearsing Schubert's "Trout Quintet" with my spouse on double bass.

In the past I would have happily done my writing late into the night, allowing my relentless hypomanic energy and obsessive tendencies to whip up an uninterrupted stream-of-consciousness manuscript with dynamic sentences and flowery language. Compulsively typing into the night and spending my days wearily and irritably coping without a recovery period would have been the romantic experience of a "crazy artist." I would have been proud. And pleased.

But that kind of experience no longer appeals to me. Instead, I took my medication on time, got to bed on time, and devoted calculated segments of my day to writing. As much as I admire people who can pour a cup of pu-erh tea and write at a standing desk until 2:00 am, or set an alarm for 4:30 am to write for five hours before daily life sets in, I have to keep my sleep and wake schedule on track. I have to take my meds, go to bed, and get my 10 hours of sedated, uninterrupted sleep. Messing with this routine can mean trouble; it can and will trigger a (usually manic) episode. I don't want to take that risk. I don't want to live like that anymore.

Knowing that I am not *actually* more creative when I exhibit manic symptoms has helped me:

- Understand that *I am creative when I am stable*, because that is just who I am. I am not creative because I am unstable.
- Not yearn to be in a manic state.
- Not think that my mania is my creativity, and vice versa.
- Understand that my ideas are just as great when I am stable; they simply *feel* different.
- Realize that it is exhausting and inefficient to function at warp speed.
- Understand that being stable does not mean I am less intelligent, boring, "slowed down," or less creative.
- Realize that I have, and am allowed to have, proportional daily ups and downs like everyone else.

And, above all: I do not romanticize mania. It is not desirable, attractive, or cute. It is actually scary. And, now, when manic symptoms present themselves, I have a treatment plan in place that looks something like this:

- I contact my psychiatrist.
- I discuss what is happening with my spouse.
- I stay home, and try to chill out.
- I take extra medication (only as directed by my psychiatrist), and go to sleep at my regular time.

My psychiatrist has been a huge support in helping me resist the seductive lure of my manic symptoms, which form a mirage of fun and fame, and to keep those symptoms in perspective. She compared a manic episode to consuming too much alcohol. It might make you feel like a better version of yourself, but you are slurring your words and can barely stand up straight.

What I want all readers to remember is this:

You are not your mania, and your mania is not what makes you creative.

CHAPTER 3

A Holistic Approach To Daily Life

Having a mood disorder often means having long-term relationships with various healthcare professionals like psychiatrists, psychotherapists, and pharmacists. These experts have given me valuable knowledge and support to understand, accept, and manage my illness. But they are not present 24 / 7, and they don't direct my daily life—I do. Living well is my primary responsibility, and one of the most important things I have learned is that the better I become at managing my day-to-day activities, the healthier and more stable I remain. I simply feel and function better when my daily life is well managed. I do not miss the bouts of frenzied energy that had me moving at warp speed, even if the world glittered and I felt like a "creative genius." I especially do not miss the crash and dark trenches of depression.

In addition to taking my medication, my stability is rooted in four things: routine, sleep, good eating habits, and regular physical movement. Interestingly enough, as I'll explain later, chronic stress, poor sleep, circadian rhythm disruption, poor nutrition and eating habits, and a lack of physical activity are also the main causes of chronic inflammation, which is linked to many illnesses, including mental illness. So, before you set out to update your lifestyle to better manage your mental wellness, consider addressing these four basic areas of your life first. While it may be tempting to purge your possessions and redecorate your home or office, these four building blocks dictate how you feel and function at the cellular level, and they will form the foundation for every other thing you do in your entire life.

ROUTINE? YES, PLEASE!

I used to think that keeping a daily routine was boring and only for people who had 9–5 jobs. The idea of going to bed at a fixed time each night and setting an alarm for the same time each morning seemed incredibly mundane. Not for me, thanks!

Now I know it is essential for me to keep a regular, daily schedule that includes taking my medication at the same time each evening, adhering to a regular bedtime, and waking up at roughly the same time each morning. My routine doesn't feel boring at all. It feels safe and reliable, because I know that when I stick to it, I will feel and function at my best. And actually, keeping a routine has *increased* my enjoyment of the activities I do each day, because the added structure I have in place to fit them in leaves me feeling great during my whole day. Each work or social activity is more gratifying and my routine keeps me rested and consistent. Just like when I practice, ensuring an organized structure gives me room for artistic freedom.

A word to freelancers: it can seem impossible at times to keep a regular routine when your work activities are all over the map. It's true that we sometimes need to adjust our hours to cater to whichever project we have on the go or accommodate fun events; however, I find that prioritizing a routine actually helps ensure that I organize my work activities in a way that supports a regular schedule.

My daily routine is about time management—how well I allocate time for work and play, as well as for rest and recovery—which in turn helps enormously with managing stress.

My life used to be an incessant series of activities, many of them happening at once or piling on top of each other. A gap in my schedule meant I needed to do more, and my work day had no boundaries. I did not allow myself time for rest and relaxation, and even prided myself on always being busy and seemingly important, thinking my constant exhaustion was worth bragging about. When someone asked "How are you?" I would boast, "Busy! Things are *insane!*"

In our go-go-go society, busyness has become a badge of honor. It gives us a sense of worth, and provides proof that we are contributing, hard-working members of society. This philosophy fits right in with the symptoms that I experienced during manic episodes, and helped reinforce how creative, accomplished, important, and effective I thought I was. Even on my most stable days I would dash from gig to gig, rehearse with intensity, and squeeze in a lesson with a cello student, always being on the move with no time to eat or catch my breath. This reflected a freelance musician's lifestyle, but I exaggerated the need to live that way.

I later learned from reading Dr. Gabor Maté[11] that for those who have been habituated to high levels of stress since early childhood, the absence of stress can leave us feeling restless, bored, meaningless and unfulfilled. I had become addicted to my own stress hormones—adrenaline, cortisol, and norepinephrine—making the rush of constant stress feel desirable. But now I understand that doing "nothing" is just as important as doing "something," and that the two need to be balanced. I finally realized that you cannot pour from an empty cup. Other working people see their evenings, weekends, and vacations as essential, so why was it not okay for me to recharge? What good was I to the communities I served if I was constantly exhausted, flustered, and burned out? I have found that a daily routine based on good time management goes a long way to reducing stress, and reducing the overall stress in my life is one of the biggest steps I can take to help myself stay well and live my life with greater ease.

Maintaining a healthy routine has required perseverance and effort, but now that I enjoy the sense of wellbeing that my routine supports, I would not want to live any other way. And although it sounds counterintuitive, I've noticed that I'm able to accomplish more and enjoy my work and life more by taking it easier.

LESS STRESS IS BEST

Along the way I have learned that stress is a key player in exacerbating inflammation and symptoms of mental illness. Every life situation—be it physical, emotional, or intellectual—makes demands on us, and we experience these demands as stressful when they seem greater than what we think we are capable of handling. Our body's stress responses are not designed to be continuously engaged. While small doses of stress can help us meet deadlines and arrive at events on time, chronic stress can increase the risks of psychological and physical health problems. Our stress hormones—adrenaline, cortisol, and norepinephrine—help us adapt in the short term, but in the long term they increase our susceptibility to issues such as anxiety, depression, digestive problems, headaches, heart disease, sleep problems, weight gain, and problems with memory and concentration.

As outlined on the Sign of the Times website[12], when we are under stress, our bodies release chemical messengers called inflammatory cytokines which send our immune system into high alert. (Inflammatory cytokines are also released when we consume a highly inflammatory diet. More on this later). Our bodies then react to stress as if it were an infection. Chronic levels of stress mean that our immune systems are working in overdrive and constantly producing an inflammatory response. This can lead to all sorts of chronic conditions, such as high blood pressure, autoimmune diseases such as multiple sclerosis, and mental illnesses.

For a person with a mental illness, problems with mood regulation make it difficult to manage emotional reactions to stress. Having challenges with information processing can get in the way of accessing the necessary coping mechanisms to deal with stressors. Stress can not only increase symptoms of a mental illness, but also affect the ability to recover.

There is good news: when I treated my condition and my mood stabilized, a virtuous cycle emerged. I gradually became more resilient to the stressors in my life, and was then better able to tackle these areas to reduce my stress levels even further. Some stressors are sudden and can't be avoided—such as a car accident or the death of a loved one—but I can lessen the effects of these stressors by managing the stressors I *can* control, and my reactions to them.

MUSIC, STILL MINE

Playing the cello has always been a part of who I am and how I express myself, but after my diagnosis, something about that clicked. While my illness was responsible for the challenges I experienced and the drive that was behind my frenzied schedule, I realized that playing music and teaching others was grounding me and connecting me mindfully with the present moment, even when my mood was unstable and my schedule was crammed. Even before I knew I had a mental illness, music was helping me treat it. When I played the cello, I was fully absorbed in every bow stroke, listening deeply to how my tone blended within an ensemble. When I was teaching, I was focused on my student and their own musical experience, as well as connecting with them musically and personally. There was no other place I could be except mindfully in that moment, which took me out of my head and away from my problems.

Treating my illness and re-thinking my schedule only made my experience of music better. I realized that music was more important to me than ever, and it had been playing a role in keeping me grounded for a long time. Since I made changes to how I approach my routine and schedule, I am able to reap the benefits of playing music even more. Now, when someone asks me how I'm doing, I can take a breath and calmly share what I am up to with a smile.

I have learned that if I don't want to burn out, I need to preserve myself. I have to develop and adhere to a realistic daily routine, one that respects not just activity but also restorative inactivity. As a freelance musician, the tendency is to say yes to every opportunity. And while I need to work to make a living and I don't always know when and what my next gig will be, I had to let go of the constant need to pack my schedule and prove how important I am by being busy. I began by gradually changing my beliefs. To do this, I applied the same discipline that I would use when learning a new piece of music: rehearsing until I feel confident and have internalized the harmony and structure. I had to believe that I was still successful and a good person, even if I wasn't running myself ragged. I had to believe that I could have a career as a musician and be a successful one, too, without making myself sick and being exhausted all the time. Like debunking the common misconception that musicians need to practice upwards of six hours a day, when shorter, focused sessions are often more effective. I started prioritizing the quality and timing of activities rather than the quantity. I simply changed my mindset, and decided I wasn't going to be "insanely busy" anymore. My plate is still full, but I can now calmly tend to one activity and then the next, with space in between. Giving my activities room to breathe allows me to enjoy the rewards of the musical path I have chosen even more, and supports my recovery by reducing my stress. I may earn a little less in a day, but my health and wellness is priceless.

SCHEDULING: I BREATHE IN BETWEEN

As part of my realistic routine, I now schedule in buffer time between appointments and activities. Each back-to-back lesson, rehearsal, or work activity has at least 15 minutes scheduled in between so I can catch my breath, make a cup of tea, and stay on top of email during business hours. I also schedule in lunch and dinner breaks, so I remember to eat. I am far more focused and effective this way, and I know my students and colleagues benefit from having me at my freshest and most relaxed.

While it may seem more efficient to book your days wall-to-wall so you can fit more in or leave work sooner, running that kind of schedule leaves you with no room to recharge or catch up if you are running behind, which has a snowball effect on stress. Some professionals may choose to book back-to-back clients to fit in the highest number of appointments, but I make a conscious effort not to. One exception is when I need to run errands, which can take a lot of time away from the activities I truly enjoy. I try to schedule errands and nonwork appointments back-to-back in the same neighborhood, so I only make one trip and efficiently use my time. I still leave buffer time for things that are time-sensitive, like a doctor's appointment, and can tag on a deferrable errand afterwards, like picking up a few groceries. The key is not rushing. This may take a little longer, but it allows me to accomplish errands without stress, and sometimes actually enjoy them. To make errands more fun and give me something to look forward to, I like to include a leisurely stroll when I can, or add-on coffee dates with friends when I am already out and about. Many birds, one outing!

The other thing I schedule is a pause day. I now take at least one day off per week—Mondays work really well, and I can often keep Fridays open as well. I try not to schedule activities before 10.00 am or after 8.00 pm, with evening performances being the exception. While I used to ask clients "What time would work best for you?" I now only offer time during *my* work hours. To keep myself organized and help me stick to my guns, I use Google Calendar, which allows me to set reminders and color-code my activities. Gigs are in bright green; regular students are in default raspberry. If a student changes their lesson time one week, I change them to yellow to alert me of the time change. Personal appointments, events or social activities are in purple. I try to make sure that each week contains some purple at a glance, to make sure I'm taking time for socializing, fun, and myself.

I block off each Monday, my chosen pause day, completely in turquoise. This ensures that I won't cave and book anything on Monday, and if I decide to, it makes me think first.

To help keep track of the little tasks, activities, and errands throughout my day that can leave me feeling overwhelmed, I also keep a small notepad to write daily lists. The night before, I write down my list of tasks for the next day, including obvious ones like "coffee," "shower," and "lunch." The next day I then check off each task, clearing my head and leaving me feeling accomplished. I'll even add new tasks, just to check them off! And each morning I make a mental note of the last activity of the day and acknowledge that that is the time when my work day *ends*.

LEARNING TO SAY NO

There is one other powerful skill I use to help maintain my routine and stay well. I have learned that I don't have to say yes to everything that comes my way. I can just say NO!

It's true that I am now in a position to be able to say no to more things because of where I am in my career, but I still feel the urge to say yes more often than I need to. The idea of saying no to anything used to be unheard of for me, especially when I was just out of school. As a young musician building a career, I couldn't yet afford to say no to work that came my way, even if it didn't pay well or didn't suit me artistically. I was groomed to believe that I would never be able to make a living as an artist, so I worked myself to the ground trying to generate as much income as possible.

I was also keeping up this constant pace out of fear. What if all of my streams of income disappeared? My work wasn't yet steady enough to trust year-round, and I feared that there could be months where I might not work at all. So, I worked even harder to make up for the possibility of times when work might be less abundant. I was also raised to be a "yes" person, and thought that saying no meant that I was negative and a party pooper, and was letting other people down. Nice girls said yes, no matter what.

While I was motivated to please others, I was also hungry for new opportunities and adventures for myself. Before I started treating my mental health, the idea of a missed opportunity would leave me in a panic. I had serious FOMO—Fear of Missing Out. What if I was missing my big break and didn't even know it? I was so ambitious that the mere idea of *anyone* else playing the gig or teaching the prospective student made me envious, so I always said yes. When anyone suggested to me that I could just say no to things that weren't as worthwhile, I thought they were nuts. Didn't they know that I had to work? I kept saying yes, yes, yes, and before I knew it I was running myself ragged, exacerbating the mental illness I didn't yet know I had. And as my career grew and I kept saying yes, one gig would lead to more. As I took on more private students and my teaching studio grew, none of my older students were leaving. My work increased, which felt exciting and filled me with pride, but I paid a price with my health.

After my diagnosis—when I had to re-think my entire lifestyle—I started to think of the quality of my projects, how each one affected my stress levels, and how they made me feel. I was fortunate to be in a position where I could support myself, so I could afford to start thinking about the kinds of projects I really wanted and what kinds of work I could realistically handle that would fit my new routine. As new performances came up, rather than respond yes right away, I took the time to really *imagine* myself doing the project. Was the opportunity and compensation worth what was being asked of me? Did it mean having to spend hours in transit, starting my day at 6 am and ending at midnight? Did it mean I wouldn't have enough time to prepare well?

Now, a project has to suit my schedule (I can be flexible when I need / want to be), be interesting to me artistically, involve other people that I want to work with, and compensate me fairly for the work involved. Some musicians refer to the "gig triangle" that consists of good people, good music, and good pay. If the project satisfies two out of three sides of the triangle, then it is worth considering!

I used to be afraid of sounding unpleasant by saying no, or potentially closing a door and losing a networking opportunity, but I have come up with different ways to politely decline while still being open to future opportunities.

When replying to a sensitive email, I always remove the recipient's email address, so I don't accidentally hit "send" too soon! For more formal correspondence, I start with a greeting ("It's great to hear from you"), followed by a note about the project ("This sounds really interesting / fun"), followed by my regrets and my reason, without going into too much detail ("I wish that I could be a part of it, but I am already committed to another service that day")—followed by a positive closing statement that leaves room for future connections ("I wish you all the best, and look forward to hearing about future opportunities to work together."). If I know the person, and want to keep it really short, this friendly reply works well: "Hi! Sounds interesting, but I'm afraid I'm already booked up that day. All the best. Hope to see you soon!" For social events that I'm truly sad to miss, I'll offer an alternative: "Why don't we meet for coffee next week instead?"

In retrospect, I realized that when I used to accept every engagement that came my way, the ones that weren't as fulfilling fooled me into feeling that I was buzzing with happiness, simply because they kept me so busy. When I started to really pay attention, these projects left me feeling weighed down with regret. I would resent the gig and end up regretting having agreed to it. Being upfront with myself about when a project or event simply isn't good for me is liberating, and it leaves space for the things I get really excited about. The empowerment I feel from preserving my own energies—and keeping my routine— confirms that I am doing what is best for me, and that I am not missing out on anything after all.

I recently learned a great approach to saying no, coined by Derek Sivers, that takes it a step further: "If it's not a *hell yes*, it's a no." This eliminates the wishy-washy feelings of a somewhat-yes. "I *guess* I could take this on ..." Life is too short, even for yes. It has to be *hell yes*. I have been applying this to the activities that come my way, and it's exciting to have so much more room for the hell yesses in my life, like a visit to the family cottage, a dedicated new student, or a great chamber music opportunity. I've learned to say no in other areas, too, to make room for hell yes: saying no to food that doesn't fuel me and make me feel amazing. Saying no to alcohol when I know it will affect the sleep I need. Saying no to staying out too late. Saying no is especially important to helping me stay well, and protecting my routine. If I don't create, stick to, and respect my own routine and boundaries, no one will.

WHY I LOVE MY SLEEP

For those of us managing a mental illness, getting adequate, quality sleep is essential, because sleep disturbances often indicate the presence of a deeper issue. Sleep also helps reduce inflammation and provides an opportunity for recovery and repair at the cellular level. Yet many of us have difficulty in this area and find sleep difficult or impossible to master.

When I was diagnosed with bipolar disorder, I was surprised to learn that maintaining what's called good "sleep hygiene" is a crucial part of treatment. Circadian rhythms dictate our sleep, waking and eating cycles, and regulate our body temperature and energy. These rhythms have a huge effect on how we feel each day. When our circadian rhythms are off, we can feel jet-lagged without having set foot on a plane.

Not getting adequate sleep affects nearly everything we do in our waking hours. It causes an inability to cope with stress, impairs our memory and concentration, makes us susceptible to mood swings, diminishes creativity and motivation, and increases our appetite due to hormonal fluctuations. For a person with a mental illness who already has challenges in these areas, a lack of sleep can have an amplifying effect.

Regulating and improving your sleep can help treat your illness, and this is how it works. When we sleep well, there are several stages that we pass through in cycles of roughly 90–110 minutes. Each stage helps repair the mind and body differently. According to tuck.com, stage one is light sleep, where you can be awakened easily. The brain settles from an active state to a state of relaxation. In stage two eye movement stops, and our bodies slow down in terms of heart rate, muscle movements, organ functions, and breath, while brainwaves become slower. Stages three and four are referred to as deep sleep, and this is when tissue growth and repair take place. Tired muscles and organs repair themselves, hormones are released, and your energy is restored. Without entering these final stages, there is little repair work that can be done[13].

The final REM (Rapid Eye Movement) stage is when our mental stresses heal themselves. This is when we dream and when our minds work hard to reconcile new information with our existing perceptions of the world. The first REM stage occurs about 90 minutes after falling asleep and recurs every 90–110 minutes thereafter, lengthening as sleep progresses. According to *Psychology Today*, "If you are unable to achieve the REM stage, you can develop severe issues with stress because your brain simply cannot adapt to the new information it is receiving. You can become overwhelmed, and a delusional breakdown can occur if you do not experience REM sleep for more than 72 hours[14]."

I used to take my sleep for granted and didn't appreciate that I wasn't really sleeping well at all. I would snack too close to bedtime, stay up late working on a stimulating project, and then I would lie with my eyes closed and travel down a wormhole, jumping from thought to thought, complete with background music. I would think that 20 minutes had passed since I lay down, and then the glow of sunrise would appear. Sleep must have happened eventually, because I would have vivid dreams that I mistook for reality and nightmares that would leave me waking in tears. But I wasn't getting adequate deep sleep, and getting out of bed in the morning was *painful*. The early risers in the house made me feel like there was something wrong with me.

This routine left me irritable and led to concentration difficulties. Of course, these were symptoms of bipolar disorder, which were made worse by a lack of sleep. And the cycle would be repeated the next night.

Now I understand what good, adequate sleep feels like. A feeling of heavy drowsiness overcomes me about 30–45 minutes after I take my medicine, and I sleep like a log through the night, with minimal tossing and turning. My sleep is deep, consistent, and undisturbed. I rarely experience racing thoughts, visions, or auditory hallucinations, and when I do, I know it's an early symptom that I might be getting unwell. My dreams are vivid and detailed, but I can wake up knowing that they were not real.

PROTECTING MY SLEEP

While my medication does a lot of the heavy lifting, I still need to take many steps to ensure that I sleep well. I have learned to *protect* my sleep. I safeguard my sleep each night and follow the steps described below on a typical work day. This list works for me, but you can adapt it to meet your own circumstances and needs.

- I try to finish eating about three hours before I go to sleep, and I start winding down at the same time each night, about 60–90 minutes before I turn out the light.
- I avoid consuming alcohol—especially close to bedtime— because it inhibits stage three sleep and beyond. While alcohol may seem to help some people fall asleep, it affects your ability to get the restorative rest you need.
- At about 8:30 to 9:30 pm, I begin to wrap up any end-of-day tasks I'm working on and commence winding down.
- At the beginning of the wind-down period (60–90 minutes before I turn out the light), I stop drinking all liquids to avoid having to get up to pee in the night.
- Cell phones, tablets, and other screens emit blue light that restricts the production of melatonin, the hormone that

signals our sleep / wake cycle. I have a program that eliminates blue light installed on all of my electronics, set to trigger at sundown. This program eliminates the blue light emitted from these devices. I do not rely on this as permission to work longer, but rather seeing the warm, hazy red screen signals that it is time to shut off electronics.

- I try to keep stress out of my bedroom. By 9:30 pm I have stopped checking email, have put my phone and laptop away, and I have reminded myself that email and other electronic tasks can wait until tomorrow. And, believe it or not, they do wait. Evening is a popular time for people to send out emails, which means that you will likely receive a few, but you don't need to reply right away. There is also the possibility that you'll open something exciting or disturbing, which will further hinder your ability to get to sleep.

- After logging off for the day, I might have a bath. The Japanese practice taking a regular ofuro (hot bath) at bedtime, which increases the release of melatonin. A hot shower works too, and through mindfulness it feels like my day is literally washing away. The warm water and evening reflection time is a great signal to my brain that it's almost time for bed. Bonus: this means I can usually get away without a morning shower.

- While my hair doesn't need washing every day, I'll wash and dry it at night time when it does. I do it before bed to maximize my sleep in the morning and help keep my morning simple and serene.

- I might watch an episode of a favorite show, depending on how I'm feeling, and only if it's not too late. I've found that this use of screens doesn't affect my sleep, partially because my medication is sedating. But sometimes a TV show feels too loud or intense, so I curl up with a book instead.

- Around 9:45 pm I take my medication. I'm careful to do this at the same time every day, and if I need to make an exception, I make sure I have extra time the next morning to sleep later. I brush and floss my teeth and pop in my mouth guard. My medication is sedating, so when I take it my "countdown" begins, and I fall asleep about 30–60 minutes after that.

- I choose pajamas that are comfortable and cozy, and get me excited about putting them on to get ready to sleep. Sometimes, if I've had a late night or two, I put my pajamas on after dinner to begin my wind-down mood even sooner.

- I make sure my room is cool and that my sheets and blankets are the ideal weight for the season: heavier in the winter, lighter in the summer. I also keep an extra blanket at the foot of the bed; if I get chilly, I can easily pull it up for extra warmth.

- I have installed blackout curtains on my bedroom window, and I unplug any glowing electronics. I also sleep with an eye mask and keep an extra mask in my travel case for use on the go. Even the smallest traces of light can disturb melatonin production and an otherwise great night's sleep, so taking care to make sure your room is dark makes a difference.

- For my mornings, I set my alarm earlier than I need, so I can take my time getting ready for the day and have some time to myself before I start work. I try to keep my alarm set for the same time each day, when possible, to stay consistent. To keep my circadian rhythm in balance, I try to get good exposure to bright, natural daylight by opening the curtains, and with a walk outdoors.

On days when I have to adjust my routine to accommodate a change in my schedule, such as a late concert (one Motown band I play with always starts at midnight), I adjust my wake time the next day so I still get an adequate amount of quality sleep. Not all careers would allow for this, of course, but freelancers like me can take advantage of our more flexible work hours to make this adaptation.

MY RULE: EAT FIRST

I've learned that our mental and physical wellbeing begins at the cellular level, and what do our cells need to perform optimally? Nutrients. From real food sources. Have you ever found yourself running from task to task, playing on your phone during the time in between appointments, and forgetting to eat altogether, or reaching for junk because *it's there*? I sure have, and it's a bad practice. If I want to feel and function at my best from one day to the next, I have to discipline myself to fuel my body and my brain at regular intervals. While there are different "regular intervals" for different people (for example some people, like me, practice intermittent fasting), the real importance lies in day-to-day consistency and routine. Eating regularly is a basic part of a holistic health plan and is especially important for those of us with mood disorders.

I've come to realize that proper and timely nutrition is essential and a non-negotiable part of my day. So important is nutrition to my new normal, that I have devoted an entire chapter in this book to my nutritional discoveries and practices. But for now, I want to highlight the importance of good eating *habits* as part of a sustaining daily routine. By this I mean eating nutritious meals at regular intervals and regular times throughout the day.

My eating habits used to be uninformed and chaotic. I oscillated between forgetfulness—getting absorbed in something and neglecting to eat at all—and obsession—craving my next snack or meal even though I'd just eaten. And craving my next snack had me reaching for choices with almost no nutritional benefits, which left me feeling hungry all over again. Never mind what I was or wasn't eating, I didn't appreciate the importance of fueling my body and brain on a regular, reliable basis. I now make eating well a priority, and if I neglect to do so, boy do I feel it.

Even an innocent deviation from my routine eating habits can be a problem. Recently, my spouse and I attended a friend's comedy show. When the show was over, our cheeks and sides were sore from laughing. Stepping out of the theatre, we noticed it was still daylight. Wanting to make the most of a "treat day" and to extend our date, we decided to indulge in a rare meal at my favorite diner—wine, a Monte Cristo with maple syrup, and sweet potato poutine—outside of my usual dinner time.

Fun though it was, our late dinner culminated in a restless night of tummy trouble and botched sleep for both of us. I woke up exhausted and foggy-headed, sluggish from my food hangover and from having taunted my meds with two glasses of wine. I was dehydrated and nutrient depleted, but my condition didn't immediately register with me.

I chugged some water, which helped me get myself together for my first cello student. But after my student left, I began lethargically scrolling my social media, silently kicking myself for not being out jogging, all the while daunted by the prospect of writing a new blog post.

Lethargic. Depleted. Unmotivated. I felt cognitively delayed and negative, negative, negative. Ugh.

Instead of struggling to type up my blog post, I reminded myself of my golden rule: EAT FIRST.

The moment the light bulb turned on, I mentally pressed "pause" and made my go-to green smoothie, two duck eggs, and wilted spinach. Vitamins, minerals, protein, and fats. I was quickly refueled and felt a heck of a lot better. Shifting my priorities was the first step; I recognized that I was nutritionally depleted and that I needed to stop and top myself up.

"You can't pour from an empty cup." This quote helps me remember to fuel myself first. As does thinking of my students, colleagues, spouse, family, and friends, and how they need me to function at my best. Although I had eaten a lot of calories the night before, I was an empty cup in terms of usable nutrients. The few nutrients in my junk meal were canceled out by the damaging, inflammatory properties of wheat, sugar, and food fried in cheap oil. By refueling with the nutrients I needed, I was quickly able to get back to functioning the way I want to.

MOVING MY WAY

Too often we think of being active as only a weight loss tool, but in my experience the mental health benefits of moving your body are enormous. Moving our bodies has been shown to reduce anxiety, depression, and stress, improve overall cognitive function, and lift negative moods—important benefits for those of us living with mental health conditions. The improvements in mood are tied to the release of feel-good brain chemicals and increased blood circulation in the brain. And, chances are you're familiar with the other benefits that accrue when you get moving: improvements in your sleep, energy, libido, endurance and mental alertness, as well as weight reduction, and positive changes in biomarkers and cardiovascular fitness. Movement gives us *mens sana in corpore sano*: sound mind in a strong body. When I started to think seriously about caring for my mental health, I identified moving my body as a way to refresh my mood, clear my mind, and feel great about myself again.

I use the term "movement" to reframe how I think about exercise. Movement can include small amounts of physical activity, like stretching or walking to the corner store. It doesn't have to mean running 10 km every day or committing to an annual gym membership, and it doesn't have to require special gear or clothing. I used to think that exercising regularly meant I had to be a weekend marathoner, a daily 5:00 am yogi, or a gym rat who worked out for hours a day. Now I know better.

Because I grew up in a family of hard-working Type A's, I was constantly trying to meet unrealistic and unsustainable expectations that didn't come naturally to me, especially with regards to exercise. I did enjoy a 30-minute jog here and there, but, honestly? I didn't want to run every day. Yet I imagined my peers effortlessly waking early each morning to go running or spending their evenings working out at the gym. I cultivated this mindset for over a decade, feeling that I had failed the moment I woke up. Every. Single. Morning. When I couldn't be up at 5:00 am to run 10 km, study, feverishly practice my cello, or otherwise be "productive" before sunrise, I trapped myself in a self-fulfilling prophecy: I was a failure. And I reproached myself throughout the day.

Now, I understand that all of this was self-imposed. Not only was I adopting a standard that I had invented for other people, but I was also trying to keep up with myself on the rare occasions when I had boundless morning energy, despite the fact that I had not slept the night before. When, in other words, I was hypomanic. I mistook those bouts of frenzied, elated energy as my normal operating speed and then beat myself up for not being able to sustain that pace all the time.

It finally dawned on me. I wasn't Type A, and I wasn't a long-distance runner. But I was interested in movement. What I could do more regularly—and what I enjoyed doing—was yoga and brisk walking. And eventually I realized that these more natural forms of movement count. I concluded that if I was walking most days, that had to be better than running once a week! Now, with every step I take, I think of my blood supply replenishing the cells in my brain and my entire being, clearing my mind and settling my thoughts.

I started my yoga practice as a teen, when I discovered an instructional video by Rodney Yee, an American yoga instructor. I was instantly hooked. (More about yoga in Chapter 7.) Yoga focused my mind and felt amazing. It made my body stronger and stilled my otherwise racing mind. It taught me to love and accept myself exactly as I was, and it connected me with the present. Ever since, yoga has been an important activity for me for the physical, mental, and spiritual benefits. Now I occasionally take classes, but more often I practice at home either alone or using an online video subscription. Even if it's been a while since my last session, I know I can always come back to my mat.

HIKE OR BIKE?

Walking is my primary mode of transportation, with cycling being my second choice, and I incorporate these activities into my day quite naturally. As much as possible, I schedule appointments and errands at locations that are close enough to walk or bike to. I chose my family doctor, psychotherapist, dentist, naturopath, chiropractor, pharmacy, and yoga studio in part because they are within walking distance. Even if I need to take public transit, I make sure I incorporate some walking. For example, instead of taking the bus I'll walk the 10 minutes to the subway station. I also try to walk in or near green space whenever possible. If my route has me walking in a straight line along a major traffic artery, I take a little extra time to discover a quieter, greener path and purposely walk through a quiet neighborhood or a park, even if it adds a few minutes to my trip. The fresh air and quieter environment help my thoughts refresh and flow with new ideas.

I have also become conscious of how much I—and we as a society—sit during the day. Naturally, I sit a lot when I teach the cello. I also sit while practicing and performing. Cellists sit with a straight back and their feet flat on the floor, but we often sit for hours at a time with a slightly twisted spine and neck. This persistent occupational sitting can wreak havoc on the body, much as it would for someone who sits at a computer all day; our bodies aren't designed to sit for hours.

Many office workers are now opting for standing or treadmill desks to combat sitting. To help counteract the effects of my sitting, I have started sitting on an inflatable stability balance disc while I'm teaching to maintain some movement in my hips and spine and strengthen my core. These balance discs are also used to help improve the focus of those with ADHD, and I've noticed an improvement in my own focus since regularly using one.

It is no secret that sitting is now said to be the new smoking, contributing to a host of chronic diseases associated with a sedentary lifestyle including heart disease, diabetes, cancer, and other conditions. We are now sitting on average 9.3 hours a day[15] (more than we are sleeping!). Even if you are physically active, the act of sitting for hours at a time every day is hard on your body, especially your heart and blood vessels, and not surprisingly, your mental health. Just like the rest of your body, your brain depends on good blood flow, too.

The psychological effects of sitting are also rooted in what we *do* when we are sitting. Are we spending eight hours a day sitting at our desk and then returning home to sit some more while we binge-watch a favorite show or plug into our social media? If depression already drains our energy and motivation, then too much time spent sitting is certainly not helping.

In addition to using a balance disc, I also make a point of standing whenever I can. Standing improves posture, tones muscles, and burns more energy, so I try to stand whenever possible. I use my buffer time between lessons to stand up and walk about, and I make sure to take my rehearsal breaks seriously and use them to move. I often eat my lunch standing up at my counter (partly because I can't be bothered to unfold the dining table) but also because it's another opportunity to stand and stretch my legs.

I MIX THINGS UP, BUT MOVE!

The main ways I get moving are through yoga, walking, and some occasional bodyweight exercises for strength training, such as push-ups and squats. These are also the ways I strengthen my body, which is extremely important. Being strong helps make everyday tasks like carting a cello around town, climbing stairs, and hauling groceries home from the store far easier. The older we get the more important strength is. It helps prevent falls, and improves recovery from injury. It also helps with body composition, which in turn improves self-esteem and mood. If I'm ever feeling down or in a rut, I always perk up after doing a set of 10 push-ups. It's a small practice, but I love how strong it makes my body feel, which in turn motivates me to keep it up, and perhaps do another set.

I don't need a gym membership, special equipment, and piles of outfits to make movement a regular part of my daily life. All I need is comfortable clothing I can move in and a supportive pair of shoes. That said, if having any of the above gets you motivated to move, then all the power to you.

In addition to physical benefits, regular movement also provides opportunities for socializing and distraction from worries. For me, moving my body promotes a feeling of self-efficacy: it boosts my self-esteem and makes me feel good in my own skin, thanks to a release of feel-good chemicals. It gives me a platform for coping with my condition in a healthy way, and promotes belief in myself and my ability to improve my life through positive changes. Because I prioritize movement and have experienced all if its benefits, I've found ways to sneak it into my day so that I get as much of it as possible. Here are some ways I get myself to move:

- **I start small.**

I might sit on the floor and stretch a bit, do a one-minute plank, or even just bring my knee up when I'm sitting, rest my foot on my other leg and let my knee fall open to do a simple hip stretch. I try to notice how each part of my body is feeling before I get moving and compare it with how I feel afterwards. This is a great time to take a moment with myself and check in. I also like taking mini-exercise breaks in order to do a few push-ups or sun salutations. Even a small amount of movement feels like hitting the personal "refresh button" and can make a big difference to my day.

- **I promise myself a coffee.**

Not a sugary carbohydrate "treat" which makes me feel ill, but something like a decaf Americano or a special tea. But first, I make myself walk all the way to the café! Having something to look forward to entices me to get out, and I soon realize that the walk was the treat all along!

- **I walk and talk!**

If you usually socialize with friends indoors or meet for a meal, mix it up by suggesting you take a stroll. Conversation can flow more easily when you talk to people side-by-side, and you'll both enjoy the fresh air and company. Nilofer Merchant even suggests walking working meetings in her TED Talk "Got a Meeting? Take a Walk"[16]. Recently I've been scheduling coffee dates where we take our coffees to go and then walk around the park. Or, if I want to try a new restaurant or café, I'll suggest to my companion that we walk there together. When I want to make a long catch-up phone call, I plug my hands-free earbuds into my phone and go on a "walk and talk" as another fun way to get moving.

- **I choose green.**

As I mentioned earlier, when I have the time, I'll choose a longer, greener path to get a lengthier stroll and to connect with nature. In the city, if I have the choice between walking underground or outside, I opt for outside.

- **I make my errands count.**

Although I try to be efficient with my errands and accomplish several at once, sometimes it is nice when errands and appointments are occasionally spread throughout the week, so I have a reason to leave the house and walk every day.

- **I'll move to a groove.**

I love walking or doing yoga with my favorite music. Yoga music, for example, doesn't have to be traditional, or sound like a spa. I love doing yoga to hits of the '60's or new singer-songwriters! I'll follow a yoga video from my online subscription and put my favorite music on my streaming service over the stereo. Have fun finding music that you really like, and you will look forward to exercising as a time to listen to what interests you. I also like to put the radio or music-streaming service on while I'm getting dressed which helps me get ready to take on the day.

- **I'll pick a podcast.**

There are thousands of great podcasts to explore, and this is an easy way to incorporate some multitasking into my day. My walk to the chiropractor is about 30 minutes each way, so I know I can listen to a one-hour episode during my walk. This has the added benefit of encouraging me to walk because I know that if I take transit, I'll miss out on the full length of the show.

- **I find a pup.**

I enjoy walks with my aunt and my girlfriend when they are walking their dogs, and reap the benefits of both the human and the canine company! It's also fun and a mood boost to chat with fellow dog-loving strangers along the path. While my home and lifestyle are not conducive to owning a dog of my own, I love the opportunity to spend time with them, and I've learned that their companionship can be wonderful for my mental health. If you think you can handle the responsibility and cost, and your building and schedule allows it, why not consider adopting a dog? They will hold you accountable for two walks daily, and are also great for meeting new people.

- **I'll join the group.**

The bipolar disorder meetup group I belong to often schedules group neighborhood strolls or hikes. I love getting outdoors with a group of like-minded folks and mixing up our meeting routine. I have always enjoyed camping and canoe trips with groups too, and there is something really special about the collegial energy of exploring nature with others. Consider joining a walking group or a nature group to help you get into the great outdoors. This is especially important if you live in a city where it can be challenging to find green space.

While sometimes I need to remind myself to move, I *always* feel better when I do, and it's now an essential part of my wellness plan.

SAFEGUARDING MY STABILITY

Living with bipolar disorder means monitoring every aspect of my day-to-day living: maintaining routines in my sleep and wake cycles, timing my medications, eating right and on time, and reducing stress. But there's one more thing: understanding and controlling my symptom triggers—those events or occurrences that can set off a chain reaction and disrupt my hard-earned stability.

A trigger is any stimulus (act, situation, event, experience, etc.) that ignites a reaction. In the case of bipolar or other mental illnesses, reactions can include depression, mania, anger or irritation, panic attacks, psychosis, suicidal thoughts, and many more.[17] Each reaction is a *symptom* of the bigger problem, the mental illness, and the trigger is the symptoms' root cause. The symptom is not the problem, the trigger is.

The holistic approach to staying well is not just about treating symptoms. Understanding and avoiding the triggers that set them off can significantly minimize symptoms or prevent them entirely. So, instead of putting out symptom fires, think about strategically *preventing* them. Cascading triggers can begin gradually, so I take note of early triggers and try to "nip them in the bud" before they escalate. Being aware of my triggers, noticing them in the moment, changing them if I can, and practicing mindfulness around them helps me the most. My current level of awareness has taken years of observing the events that lead to episodes of mania and depression, but my efforts have been well rewarded.

One of my triggers is consuming too much alcohol, a stimulating indulgence that can release other triggers in a snowball effect. I'm not supposed to drink at *all* on the medication I take, but there are other reasons that I abstain. Drinking alcohol usually involves socializing and lowers inhibitions, with the result that I can get overstimulated (trigger) and stay up far later than my usual bedtime, messing up my sleep schedule (another trigger). Not only does consuming alcohol encourage me to stay up too late, but alcohol itself affects the *quality* of my sleep, and this leaves me feeling even worse than just tired the next day. Even two drinks screw me up, impairing my cognition, concentration and mood. Sometimes I need several days to recover from one botched night, and if I'm not careful, a single incident of social drinking can trigger an episode of mania.

Recently I indulged too much at a friend's wedding—the cherry on top of a week of summer holiday where my eating, drinking, and sleeping habits had already been relaxed. The night of the wedding I had just three drinks, and was even sipping water in between, but it was still too many. I turned in too late, tossed and turned all night without a wink, and woke up not only congested and with a sore throat, but also irritable and delirious. I could feel an episode of hypomania brewing, and this was the day before I had to go to Cleveland for a show.

You can see how one trigger can lead to another, then another. I control my alcohol consumption by only having one drink, and I only allow myself that drink if it is early in the evening so that the alcohol is out of my system by the time I take my medication. I have learned to enjoy drinking non-alcoholic beverages at social functions, and I prioritize getting home in time for a good night's sleep. I know now that my wellness is more important than staying out late and having too much alcohol.

Traveling is another one of my triggers and is a common stressor for many, even those who do not have a mental illness. Just the upheaval of leaving my stable home contributes to my feeling of stress even if I'm going somewhere relaxing like the family cottage. First, there is the lead-up of planning and rearranging my work schedule to accommodate the travel. Then there is the stress of being in a new place and leaving my daily comforts behind. Other factors include sleeping in a new bed, jet lag if changing time zones, and having to acclimatize to a new schedule start time if traveling for work. These elements can all destroy my hard-earned sleep routine, but I minimize the disruptive effects with lots of planning, preparation, and scrupulous self-care, and by allocating extra time to acclimatize to my new environment.

When I was asked to travel to Taiwan to perform in a music theatre production, my psychiatrist recommended that I don't go at all! The time change was severe: 12 hours. Day would become night, and night would become day. Recovering from a three-hour time change takes me a week! My saving grace was that

I was only going to be there 10 days—not long enough to truly acclimatize and risk also being affected on the other end when I returned home. I armed myself with ammunition: I brought emergency-only medication just in case, and followed my travel plan to a T, including timing my medication strategically. It worked! The trip was a huge undertaking, but ended up being successful and a great experience.

I know from experience that it is not possible to avoid every event or occurrence that threatens my stability, and even if it were possible to eliminate them all, it would make my life extremely dull. Furthermore, I recognize that many triggers are beyond my control. The important thing is to identify the ones that I am most susceptible to and to take care to monitor and manage those that affect me the most. This requires me to foster self-knowledge and insight and to develop planning and coping strategies that lessen the blow of stressors that can trigger my mental illness.

If you suffer from depression, anxiety, bipolar disorder, or schizophrenia, you likely have a unique mix of triggers that are personal to you and that can cause you to destabilize. And, while some triggers are specific for certain types of mental illness, many triggers are common to all. Triggers can negatively impact healthy individuals, but for someone with a mental illness, they can mean the difference between functioning well each day and becoming seriously ill.

Here is a list of common, general triggers that I have assembled (with the help of *Loving Someone With Bipolar Disorder* by John D. Preston and Julie A. Fast[18]). Some of them apply to me, and some might be relevant to you:

- Alcohol consumption
- Arguments
- Believing and engaging in negative self-talk
- Constantly doing tasks with no down time, or being constantly on the move

- Caffeine consumption
- Caring for a sick relative
- Change, generally speaking
- Changing or stopping medication, especially without a doctor's consent
- Cluttered living space
- Consuming an unhealthy diet, low in nutrients and high in refined foods
- Deadlines
- Death of a loved one
- Driving in bad traffic
- Drug use, including medications
- Excess stimulation, like parties, crowded malls or shopping centers
- Spending time with high-maintenance or unstable people
- Holidays, especially including travel, stressful family interactions, food and drink, or spending temptations
- Hunger or dehydration
- Indulging in too much stimulating junk food
- Lack of a schedule or structure
- Lack of movement or exercise
- Lack of self-awareness and insight
- Living an overly stimulating lifestyle, and spending time with people who follow one
- Media and following stressful world events
- Over-scheduling or overcommitting
- Saying yes too often, and taking on too much
- Social events and occasions
- Social media overuse
- Strained relationships with spouse, family, friends, coworkers
- Too many obligations
- Travel, time changes, and jet lag

- Unhealthy sleep habits: irregularity, staying up too late, or sleeping all day
- Watching violent movies, television shows, video or computer games
- Work-related stress and obligations

CHAPTER 4

Nutrition

As a person who manages a mood disorder, I am passionate about nutrition because I have learned that what I eat affects my entire being and nourishes every cell in every part of my body, including my brain. Notice that I use the term "nutrition," not "diet." Nutrition means more than a list of specific foods that should or should not be eaten. It includes the things that you eat, what they contain, how they interact with each other, how the body makes use of them, and how often and how much is enough. The way you manage your nutrition can set you up for feeling your absolute best or leave you sluggish, irritable, constantly hungry, and tired from sleepless nights. Poor nutrition can also put you at risk for disease.

In treating mental illnesses such as depression and bipolar disorder, the focus of traditional medicine is on repairing an imbalance of neurotransmitters in the brain through medication. Experience has convinced me that the right medication is critically important to my health, but I am also interested in functional medicine, which looks at underlying causes and promotes the optimal functioning of the body and its organs. Functional medicine asks how those neurotransmitters became imbalanced in the first place. Or, more specifically, what if mental illnesses were to be seen as a symptom of other underlying problems?

Disclaimer: I am not a health or nutrition expert. The information provided in this section is a compilation of well-researched facts and general principles that I have used to help inform my own self-experimentation in the area of nutrition. I have spent years fine-tuning what I eat, when I eat, and how I eat. What I have discovered works best for me, might not work best for others. Self-experimentation and patience are key to figuring out what does work for you. So, please talk to your doctor and a nutrition consultant before making any changes to your nutrition plan or lifestyle. Start by making small changes and see how your mind and body respond.

MY NUTRITIONAL LEARNING CURVE

Before I was diagnosed with bipolar disorder I had poor nutrition, but I didn't know it. Nor did I understand how my bad choices and bad habits were contributing to poor mental health.

When I was a child I had easy access to refined foods, even though my family thought that our eating was "healthy." We had different concepts and ideas of "healthy eating" in the '90's and I remember often bemoaning that we weren't allowed any "treats." There was always plenty of low-fat milk, juice, hot chocolate mix, and Ovaltine in the house. The default breakfast foods that I grew up on included sugar-filled instant oatmeal and cereal, toast and bagels with sugary spreads, muffins, pancakes and waffles with syrup, fruit and juice. Not to mention occasional breakfast "treats" (that aren't all that different) like cinnamon buns, Pop-Tarts and Toaster Strudels. It's amazing that we considered this food at all, let alone a viable option for starting the day.

As a teenager, before sprinting out the door in the morning, I'd often have powdered "instant breakfast" mixed with milk (a combination with more corn syrup solids than vitamins) because, otherwise, I wouldn't have eaten anything at the start of my day. But by mid-morning I had trouble concentrating in class, was exhausted and foggy-headed, and pined for candy bars. The sugary drink that started my day left me craving more.

As an adult I associated eating with craving. My meals consisted mostly of carbohydrates with an emphasis on bread and grains. Breakfast was toast with jam or cinnamon sugar and butter, a muffin, cereal or a pastry. Lunch was a bagel with cream cheese or a limp sandwich. And dinner was pasta or a rice-based curry with naan bread. No matter what, I had to have bread.

At the time I didn't know that some gastrointestinal problems are associated with mood disorders, but I experienced a host of symptoms. I had bloating and gas all day, every day. I got irritable and ravenously "hangry" (hungry and angry) and had to eat *now* or heads would roll! I would satisfy my desperate need for food with carbohydrates, sugar, or both, and experience a high—only to be hungry and irritable 30 minutes later. On top of the bloating, gas, constipation, and irritability, I had brain fog and eczema and almost always had an acne breakout. As soon as one blemish would heal, another would emerge.

My irritability, thought to be a "teen thing," was a symptom of untreated bipolar disorder—I know that now—but my eating habits sure weren't helping. Could my diet have been contributing to my mental illness? I often thought about taming my sweet tooth a little, but other than that, I believed I was eating "normal" food, so I should be fine. I didn't recognize that I was addicted to carbohydrates. And what I didn't know was that the refined grains that made up so much of my diet were really empty calories. Inside my body they were processed like sugar, and they had a similar effect on my blood sugar; it was as if I was eating sugar!

Yet, the idea of meals without starchy carbs or grains was unthinkable. Wouldn't I be *hungry* without them? Didn't they "fill me up"? And, wasn't I making wholesome choices when I selected what was described on the packaging as "whole grain" bread, bagels or pasta? Nope.

When I finally learned about nutrients (and that refined carbohydrates contain very few), a lightbulb went on: I wasn't being fully nourished, and my body was telling me so by producing feelings of hunger 30 minutes after I ate, among other side effects.

In my research I learned that some nutrients specifically support better mental health, tackle depression, and improve mood, such as calcium, chromium, folate, iron, magnesium, omega-3 fatty acids, vitamins B6 and B12, vitamin D, and zinc. Without consuming these essential nutrients from protein, vegetables and good fat, my own nutrition left a lot to be desired.

My carb-based choices meant I was not getting the macro- and micronutrients my body needed to function at its best. Worse yet, I may have unknowingly been contributing to disorders in my body and brain and exacerbating inflammation, an immune system response, by what I was feeding my gut. It was only when I developed gastric reflux from extreme stress that I started to look at my diet more closely. And, once I was diagnosed with bipolar disorder, I knew I had to make big, lasting changes.

After many failed "diet" attempts such as just eating salad, I knew I was in for habit changes as opposed to temporary fixes. I needed enduring, lifelong change based on research, knowledge, and trial and error. I proceeded slowly, in small steps, with many failures along the way. But gradually I transformed my eating from a high-carb, low-nutrient regimen to a protein, vegetable, and fat-based one, and I broke my sugar and carb addiction. I'm so passionate about the result of putting nutrition first that I want to share my discoveries so others can benefit from my experience as they see fit.

TAMING MY CARB ADDICTION

Nutrition is a hot topic these days. We all want to know what to eat to be healthier, improve body composition, avoid disease, and live longer. And we're looking for an easy answer, something we can do today that will show results tomorrow. This has led to a parade of media headlines that point to simple solutions. Eat more fruits and vegetables! Avoid trans fats! Drink red wine! Eat chocolate! Nutritional dogma is rampant, confusing, and frustrating.

Nutrition is too nuanced and individual to be reduced to one-size-fits-all information, and the science that forms the basis of nutrition studies can be dubious; it is difficult to conduct proper, controlled experiments. The results can be based on selective information and presented in such an authoritative and convincing way that, as a layperson, it's difficult to even imagine an opposing view.

So I relied on basic, established facts to inform my nutritional journey. I learned that fat accumulation is triggered by the hormone insulin, and the release of insulin is triggered by elevated levels of blood glucose—the result, for instance, of my instant breakfast drinks. When faced with a sharp elevation of blood glucose, the pancreas tends to overshoot and releases more insulin than needed, which in turn gets rid of too much glucose. This leads to a suboptimal drop in blood glucose levels that trigger hunger. In other words, my refined carbohydrate diet would cause my blood sugar levels to spike up and then drop down dramatically. Fluctuations like these can create a vicious cycle that may lead to insulin resistance, chronically elevated blood sugar, and eventually, metabolic syndrome and type 2 diabetes.

And potentially more concerning for me was the recent link between chronically elevated blood sugar levels and brain health. For example, above-normal blood sugar levels have been associated with an increased risk of developing dementia, leading some people to refer to Alzheimer's disease as "type 3 diabetes." So, for overall brain health, it seemed best to avoid elevated and dramatic fluctuations in my blood glucose levels. Translation: I had to tame my sweet tooth for the long term and take a deeper look at what the carbohydrates I was addicted to were actually doing to my body—and my brain.

I found that a good first step in controlling my blood glucose level was to remove foods from my diet that tended to have the greatest effect on it. In other words, emphasizing what are known as low glycemic foods, those carbohydrates that are more slowly digested, absorbed and metabolized and that result in a slower rise in blood glucose. The Glycemic Index is a way to rank foods based on how they affect blood glucose levels. As a general principle, the more refined a carbohydrate is, the more quickly it elevates blood glucose and the higher its glycemic index. But all carbohydrate will raise blood glucose to some extent.

Don't get me wrong. I still love to eat, but I now get even more enjoyment out of knowing that I have fed my cells the nutrients that my body needs to function at its best. I'm protecting my brain. My dental check-ups have improved. And I feel much, much better.

THE GUT AND THE BRAIN. WHO'S IN CHARGE?

While I was treating my gastric reflux, I was fascinated to learn that science is beginning to give us insights into the relationship between the digestive system and the brain. For example, accumulating evidence suggests that microscopic organisms in our gut not only regulate what goes on in our intestines, but may also regulate brain function and behavior.

From the surface of our skin to the inside lining of our guts, over 100 trillion organisms live on or in our bodies. These organisms, known together as the microbiome, outnumber the cells in our bodies 10 to one, and our bodies cannot function without them[19]. Most of the microbiome is found within the gut and is composed of microorganisms such as eukaryotes, fungi, bacteria, and viruses. A two-way communication occurs between the central nervous system (consisting of the brain and the spinal cord) and the enteric nervous system (that governs the function of the gastrointestinal tract). Research[20] indicates that the gut microbiota influences these communications, with back-and-forth signaling along neural, endocrine, immune, and other connections.

The microbiome works with our bodies to keep *all* of our systems functioning properly. It not only keeps our digestive systems functioning, but also assists with regulating our immune responses. If the digestive system is vulnerable to changes in the microbiome, so too is the immune system, and shifts in the composition or density of the microbiome—such as those due to dietary changes or antibiotic use—can impact immunity and inflammation in our bodies.

When parts of our bodies experience trauma or are exposed to foreign organisms such as bacteria and viruses, our immune systems have a natural protective response called inflammation, a process where the body's white blood cells and other substances protect us from infection. Symptoms of inflammation can include swelling, stiffness, headaches, fatigue, and loss of energy. Sometimes there are no bacteria or viruses to fight off, but the immune system triggers an inflammatory response nonetheless, causing the body to respond as if normal tissues are abnormal or infected. Certain foods can contribute to this "misdirected" inflammation, and dietary inflammation—caused by eating a diet rich in inflammatory foods—is a chronic condition that has been linked to many types of cancer, cardiovascular disease, type 2 diabetes, and more recently, depression and bipolar disorder.

According to a journal article entitled "The Microbiome, Immunity, and Schizophrenia and Bipolar Disorder" (Dickerson, Severence, Yolken, 2017), research has recently summarized connections between the human microbiome, schizophrenia and bipolar disorder, and studies have found increased gastrointestinal inflammation in those with either condition[21]. Other studies have shown an association between an increased incidence of psychiatric disorders and the receipt of antibiotics that may have altered the microbiome. Evidence also links schizophrenia and bipolar disorder to sensitivities to gluten and lactose, which can both lead to inflammation.

So, what can we do to keep our microbiomes functioning optimally and reduce inflammation in our bodies?

I AM WHAT I EAT

Reading as much as I could about bipolar disorder, I was surprised to learn about a link between chronic inflammation—especially that of the brain—and mental and behavioral health disorders such as bipolar disorder, depression, anxiety, schizophrenia, OCD, ADHD and autism spectrum disorder. There is now a well-established connection in research between inflammation and bipolar disorder, and new discoveries are being made each day. According to the journal article *Inflammation in Depression and the Potential for Anti-inflammatory Treatment* (Köhler, Krogh, Mors, Benros, 2016) research subjects who were given toxins that provoke inflammation experienced depressive symptoms, and in other research, inflammatory markers normalized when clinical depression subsided[22]. So, how is inflammation connected to mental illness?

When our bodies have an inflammatory reaction, chemicals called cytokines are excreted from immune cells, and those that promote inflammation—inflammatory cytokines—generate a wide variety of psychiatric symptoms, including depression. Recent research[23] links immune and inflammatory mechanisms to the symptoms and underlying causes of bipolar disorder, with the main finding being an increase in the levels of inflammatory cytokines. When a person is experiencing an acute episode of bipolar disorder, researchers have found elevated levels of inflammatory cytokines along with the activation of the glial cells, brain cells that surround and support neurons. These changes lead to neuroinflammation—inflammation of the nervous system that includes the brain and spinal cord.

The conventional medical belief is that, as with depression, a chemical imbalance in the brain causes bipolar disorder, and medication is needed to repair the imbalance. This is certainly true; my medication allows me to function normally and has treated my manic and depressive episodes with lifesaving effect. However, I'm convinced that addressing the underlying roots of my illness through improved nutrition, especially when research suggests a link between gut health and mental health, is another necessary step. I prefer a holistic approach to treating my mood disorder. For me, medication is essential for treating mental illness acutely, but to make holistic changes in the long term and treat the source, I thought it necessary to address the chronic inflammation and immune system activation that, according to the research, is a major underlying cause of mental and behavioral afflictions.

I learned that the main culprits of chronic inflammation are a lack of diversity in the gut microbiome, GI infections, chronic stress, lack of physical activity or too much intense physical activity, circadian rhythm disruptions, chronic infections, toxins that have accumulated in the body, and dietary inflammation, which is inflammation induced by food intolerances and/or eating what's become known as the Standard American Diet (SAD!), a nutrient-poor diet rich in foods that promote inflammation.

So, what foods are highly inflammatory? The main offenders are carbohydrates, especially refined carbohydrates like sugars and flours, and certain fats, including trans fatty acids and omega-6 fatty acids (found in vegetable oils).

MY "AHA!" MOMENT

Bingo. For nearly 30 years and on a daily basis, my brain had been affected by highly inflammatory foods that were having a negative impact, and were likely contributing to my bipolar symptoms. The neuroinflammation was the byproduct of my diet. The refined carbohydrates I consumed gave me that satisfying high, but had me crash into irritability soon after. And who knows how inflammation was affecting my brain in the long term? Surely there was a link to my bipolar disorder. I needed to start taking care of my brain, and that had to include what I was feeding myself. New eating habits would help heal my brain. Could I eat my way to mental wellness?

MY NEXT STEPS ... AND THEN ...

I also badly wanted to be free from constantly craving sugar—and the spike / crash rollercoaster of my blood glucose—so I could focus on other activities instead of wondering when I could eat next. Too much of my focus and energy was going toward my next snack or meal. Plus, feeling ravenous all the time was inconvenient and distracting.

Several research sources[24] suggest that people with mental illnesses have improved their symptoms through a diet rich in vegetables, protein, and good fats, basically emphasizing a nutrient-dense, anti-inflammatory diet that focuses on the foods that humans have been eating for the majority of our evolutionary history—those that we are well adapted to and our bodies know how to process.

I decided to try the nutritional practices suggested by my research, with a simple emphasis on high-quality meat and fish, fresh fruits and vegetables, and nuts and seeds. My changes started in small ways and developed gradually, so I would not face the feeling of withdrawal and deprivation that could lead to failure or slow me down. I also incorporated some basic principles into my nutritional practices. I decided that I would eat as many *nutrients* as I could and, as much as possible, choose fresh produce that was recently living. To the extent that I could, I would also eat organic food, especially selections from what the Environmental Working Group calls the "Dirty Dozen," a list of the 12 most pesticide-laden fruits and vegetables. And if I couldn't find organic, I would try to emphasize what they call the "Clean 15." I treated all sugars the same, knowing that—whether they were refined or natural—they would cause inflammation and the release of insulin.

I began to read food labels and look for products containing as few ingredients as possible. I was mindful of ingredients like wheat, gluten, dairy, or sugar that can have a negative effect on the gut, and embraced fermented foods like sauerkraut and nutrient-dense bone broth to heal and promote my gut health. I also paid attention to what I ate at different times of the day. I stopped starting my day with a sweet breakfast—even a fruit-based one—because I wanted to protect against cravings for the entire day. I stopped eating at least three hours before bedtime. And I kept food in perspective by testing my need for it, asking, "Am I *really* hungry? Am I hydrated? How nutritious was my last meal? Can I wait a little longer?"

I progressed in stages, and here is what I developed as routine nutritional practices. A reminder, however: do not start a new way of eating before consulting a specialist who is informed about nutrition. What works for me may not be right for you.

- **I began by not buying bread.**

This had practical benefits, too: it took a long time for our household of two to eat through a loaf of bread, and it would often go stale or moldy by the time we got to the end. No more! Morning toast or cereal was replaced by delicious, filling, leafy green and berry smoothies, or eggs with veggies.

- **I switched the fruit I ate.**

I stopped buying starchy, sugary bananas every week and replaced them with lower glycemic fresh or frozen berries or, occasionally, apples, but only as a treat.

- **I swapped my fats**.

I stopped using omega 6–rich vegetable oils like corn, soybean, and canola, which promote inflammation. For cooking, I use rendered fat from quality, healthy animals, butter from grass-fed cows or coconut oil, and for salad dressings I use extra virgin olive oil.

- **I walked the grocery circle.**

I stopped going down the middle aisles at the grocery store and now I go around the perimeter instead. The inner aisles contain the packaged food "products" that are often manufactured with dozens of mystery ingredients. My new approach makes grocery shopping so much simpler, too. Nutritional minimalism!

- **I stopped buying milk and substitutes.**

I used to buy non-dairy milk replacements like almond or soy milk, but it was too difficult to find them without sweeteners or other additives, so it was simpler to just not buy milk. I quickly lost a taste for it, too—even in coffee and tea!

- **I upgraded my baking.**

When I bake for special occasions, I now make whole-food desserts from a base of nut and nut flours, coconut and coconut flours, and sweetening that comes from fruit, dates, or a bit of maple syrup or dark chocolate.

- **I redefined my "treats."**

I love occasional treats as much as anyone, but I redefi ned my idea of a treat to quality items that didn't make me feel ill or threaten my wellness. Instead of something like a traditional box of cookies or half a cake, my occasional treat list now consists of things like a decaf Americano, a piece of quality dark chocolate, a couple of dates or a bowl of berries, a grain-free brownie, or a rare slice of cashew-based "cheesecake"—one of my favorite things to make!

Here is what happened when I decided to meet my body's nutritional needs in a way that was new and different for me:

- **I was amazed that I stopped feeling hungry between meals.**

I was finally giving my body the nutrients it needed, fuel that it could use: vitamins, minerals, amino acids (protein) and fat. Our brains are made of *fat*. Fat was my friend.

- **Eating suddenly became dead simple.**

Protein, vegetables, and fat. I loved not having to buy so many *products*. I applied minimalism to my grocery shopping.

- **I started to feel amazing.**

When I started eating mostly protein, vegetables and fat, I started to feel fantastic. I actually "felt" lower inflammation in my entire body. My mood was more even-keeled and I was sleeping better, which improved my mood even more. I could focus more easily, my skin stopped having itchy flare-ups and didn't feel so reactive, and I felt less puffy overall. I also slimmed down by a good 10 lbs. That had not been my goal, but I welcomed this side effect.

- **My digestion regulated.**

No more gas, bloating, and constipation.

- **My skin cleared.**

My eczema healed and disappeared entirely, especially as my stress levels reduced too, and I stopped breaking out. My skin finally stayed clear and developed a glow, which gave me even more confidence.

- **I noticed the difference when I went back.**

I was less irritable and reactive, but I noticed all of these symptoms return as soon as I'd "cheat" with a carb-loaded meal or a sugar binge, thinking "once in a while" was okay.

- **I beat hanger.**

I lost the desperate cravings that carbs gave me. It took time, but I broke my addiction. Instead of feeling ravenous before meals, I now just feel a subtle hunger.

- **I can live without much sweetness.**

I still love "treats" and have them often, but the categories are smaller and my standards are high. When I don't overload on sugar every day, a piece of fruit tastes really, really sweet! And since I overcame my addiction, I find it easy to go days without anything sweet at all.

I never tire of eating protein, vegetables, and fat, and there are so many ways you can keep this trio interesting.

I can't emphasize how thrilled I am with my new nutritional practices. They are easy to carry out and they make me feel so alive. I love that I am helping promote my mental wellness from the inside out.

CHAPTER 5

Minimalism for Mental Health

Since being diagnosed with bipolar disorder, I have intentionally chosen stability over spells of frenzied, elated energy where the world sparkles and glitters. Feeling great actually feels *better* than feeling mind-blowingly magnificent and believing I am super-human. I am now free of my debilitating depressions, and manic episodes no longer have any allure. I am still a colorful, creative person. To sustain my new normal, I avoid excess stimulation and am mindful of triggering events or occurrences that could threaten my hard-earned peace. I have changed my behaviors and my attitudes, and I energetically protect my daily routine. But what I haven't yet explained is the philosophy that informs and underpins the daily life I have developed post diagnosis. That philosophy is called minimalism.

I became interested in minimalism when I started to notice how profoundly well I felt after tidying my home. Every piece of clutter I removed—every pile I consolidated—had the same effect on my *mind*. Like telling the truth, it was unburdening. I call it "freeing up brain space." Little by little, I started applying a minimalist approach to all of my possessions, including personal care and cleaning products and my wardrobe. Over time the philosophy permeated my work life, organization, and finances as well.

Minimalism focuses on enhancing our lives through what we *remove* from them, rather than what we add. Additions often come in the form of clutter, which doesn't really make us happier and which we don't need. A minimalist lifestyle is one of reduced stimulation. I admit into my life only those things that I have identified as worthy of my time and attention. My willingness to do this is an indication of how precious my overall stability is to me.

There are many wonderful books and articles on the power of minimalism and its effect on mental health and wellbeing. Joshua Becker, at the website "Becoming Minimalist," describes this way of life as "the intentional promotion of the things we most value and the removal of everything that distracts us from it." In keeping with this attitude, and to the furthest extent possible, my life now emphasizes activities and possessions that provide reliable support; it excludes clutter and anything in excess that threatens me with instability.

PERSONAL CARE AND CLEANING: LESS IS NO SACRIFICE

I began by tackling my army of personal care and cleaning products. At first I was merely seeking healthier and cheaper options and to reduce my exposure to toxins, but along the way I discovered that minimizing the products I use every day dramatically cleared my mind. As a result, I decided I could no longer live with the city of plastic bottles in my shower, my junk pile of uni-tasking cosmetics, or the cascade of cleaning products littering my kitchen and bathroom. When I connected to the way I felt, the clutter overwhelmed me and made me feel frantic, claustrophobic, and overstimulated. If I ran out of something, the branded packaging urged me to buy more, adding yet another product or potion to my shopping list. I was always *acquiring*, filling an imaginary void, and looking for solutions to problems I didn't have. Did I really need five different moisturizers for my body, feet, hands, face *and* eyes?

Simplifying my personal care has made living with bipolar disorder, and life in general, a whole lot easier. Using multitasking, cost-effective, nontoxic products with fewer ingredients that I rarely need to buy has freed up my mental energy, giving me a better chance to thrive. Some of these I even make myself, turning personal care into a creative space and money-saving activity I enjoy. Paring down my collection of products has given me room to breathe mentally, physically, and spiritually.

RESISTING RETAIL THERAPY

As a person who follows minimalist guidelines, I reject the notion that shopping is the route to happiness. I need to exercise caution when shopping in order to make sensible purchases and save money. And I need to be alert to the seduction of advertising and how my mental wellbeing is impacted by the illusion of happiness created by buying things.

While our societal buying culture is changing in some circles, I grew up in a consumerist culture that valued stuff over experiences. Holidays were celebrated and love was shown by giving objects. New "stuff" and physical needs were favored over emotional needs and experiences. (Thankfully, this improved as I got older.) I used to shop for weekend recreation and entertainment, make purchases on impulse, and easily fall prey to enticing advertising. As a newly independent and fancy-free university student, I didn't see the irony in purchasing entire DVD sets of favorite shows like *Sex and the City* on impulse. In retrospect, it's comical that the purchase left me feeling even more empowered and entitled to buy what I wanted. I was seduced by eBay auctions, campus poster and gadget sales, and many cute, impractical shoes. Why couldn't an undergraduate student shop like Carrie, Miranda, Samantha and Charlotte?

Seeing a new outfit on a mannequin, a trendy throw-cushion, or a cute knick-knack in a magazine created a feeling of need. Each item promised happiness and completion. If I had that dress, I would be just like the perfect model in the ad, and if I bought that set of storage containers, my chaotic life would transform into the epitome of organization. From the moment I swiped my credit card, my brain would light up with euphoria and feel-good chemicals—I could buy a better me!—while I ignored my declining credit limit.

But a day later the spark would die out, and I'd go back to feeling the way I always did—not quite complete. Not "enough." I would already be seeking my next high, and so my credit card abuse continued. In less than one week, while at university, I ate out or had drinks at 13 different restaurants! Working part-time at a pub and teaching a few lessons each week made my spending worse, because I felt entitled to spend what I had worked hard to earn. I made excuses like "I just got paid," "I'll be getting paid soon so I'll make it up," "I didn't spend much *that* time, so I can afford to now," or "I still have __ days before I need to pay my __ bill." I was lucky that I was so young that my available credit was relatively low.

Later, in my twenties, I earned a sizable lump sum that I now wish I had invested more wisely. Instead, I impulsively commissioned a vibrant royal blue cello made of near-indestructible carbon fiber. I had obsessed and schemed about that instrument for weeks and justified it as being something I needed. It was the most expensive thing I had ever purchased. But the love affair was short; after a while, the shine wore off. The cello's sound wasn't what I really wanted. I eventually purchased another carbon fiber cello, a better one that superseded the royal blue cello as my biggest-ever purchase. *That* cello was the one I should have bought in the first place! *It* had the sound I wanted. I now found myself with two carbon fiber instruments—one more than I really needed. As a step toward living my new, minimalist lifestyle, I eventually sold the blue cello to someone who appreciates it, and I used the proceeds to pay off my line of credit.

For many people with bipolar disorder, impulsivity is a major symptom. And for a lot of people, this can mean serious, debilitating impulse spending that racks up debt and wipes out life savings. Fortunately, my impulsivity has been limited to relatively low-cost items, but my purchases still added up. Meanwhile, clutter would grow around me like weeds and overwhelm my ruminating mind. Physical clutter fed my mental clutter, and my mental clutter was augmented by a stream of advertising messages. After my diagnosis, it dawned on me that I often couldn't think straight or focus and felt overwhelmed because I was surrounded by the constant push to buy more, to be more, and to value stuff. Now I know that I need to guard against the negative messaging and constant stimulation of advertising. I finally recognize that I have enough and I *am* enough.

I also eventually realized that most of my stuff was not directly tied to my happiness, yet it stimulated my mental chatter. As I began to navigate my illness I was driven to change my environment, and decided to remove everything from my life that seemed to be making it worse. As I explored minimalism, I noticed a big shift in how I felt when I would purge my closet and give things away. I felt physically lighter and relieved by having freed up room to think and breathe. I had more brain space. More clarity. I wasn't free of my illness, but without the constant stimulation of the unnecessary stuff that surrounded me, I was able to focus on my treatment and enjoy my *life*, not my stuff.

Through deep self-reflection and psychotherapy, I explored the sources of my feeling "not enough" and the impulse to self-medicate with binge shopping, eating, drinking, and other behaviors. Looking inward, I was able to mend emotional pain and strengthen my self-esteem. After years of doing this deeply personal work, I feel stronger than ever, and I am able to resist the allure of buying because I no longer feel that I am lacking.

Now, when I decide that I need to buy something beyond the bare necessities and it can't be borrowed, rented, or sourced second-hand, I take a bit of extra time researching, to find just the right item at an appropriate price point that meets my needs exactly. I think about its afterlife. How will I store it? How long will

I have this? How much space is this going to take up, physically and mentally? And I think about how privileged I am to be able to make each purchase. I don't allow myself to buy things on impulse anymore. When impulsivity strikes, I take the extra step to remind myself that I was fine before and I'll be okay without the item.

I recently made the now-biggest purchase of my life, investing some of my savings in the instrument of my dreams. Using the money I saved by not going out for dinners or buying cheap outfits, I was able to purchase a beautiful French cello, 100 years older than I am with a fantastic sound. It is a joy to play. Its big, warm sound is essentially my brand, and I was at a point in my career where it made sense to invest in an instrument of this caliber. Instruments like these usually appreciate, and after I took the time to research the maker and inspect the cello, I knew that it was a good investment. My cello is also the tool I use to earn my livelihood every single day, so the cost-per-use is quite low!

Sure, we all need to shop sometimes, and it can be fun to buy things that excite or please us on occasion. But as a person with a mental health condition, I can't surrender my wallet—or my mind—to someone else. I need to monitor and manage the urge toward excessive, emotionally driven impulse spending.

Here are the questions I ask myself before making any purchase. It may seem like a long list, but asking even a few of these questions reinforces my ability to spend wisely and save money. These questions also help me make sure that I am not unconsciously responding to a manufacturer's advertising or falling prey to retail therapy.

- Am I buying this impulsively?
- Am I only tempted to buy this because it's on sale? An even *better* deal would be not buying anything!
- Can I find it cheaper elsewhere?
- Can I make or borrow this?

- Can it wait? I force myself to take some time to think: I sleep on it, or give myself a few days or a week before making a decision. Like I mentioned in the nutrition section, I take a moment to breathe before reaching for an impulsive treat.
- Does this item have long-term use or will it quickly become obsolete?
- Do I really need this?
- Do I want to buy this because I feel happy, sad, bored, etc.?
- Do I already have something just like it?
- For food items: is it a part of my grocery list or am I reaching for a snack I don't actually need?
- Is it better or different from everything I own? If it's better, what will I do with the item I already have? If it's different, why do I need it?
- Is it high quality? Buying quality may mean a higher price tag, but if it lasts a long time, it will mean a lower cost-per-use and increase the chance that it won't need to be replaced.
- Is it trendy and likely to go out of style eventually?
- Is it a uni-tasker or multitasker?
- What is the cost-per-use or cost-per-wear of this item, and does that figure make sense? For example, if it's a $500 dress and I wear it twice, it will cost me $250 each wear!
- Would I *rent* this for this price? For cheap or disposable items, I like to reframe the purchase price, and think of it as the *rental* price, knowing I won't have it forever. Imagining I am renting the item usually stops me from buying it.

Finally, a statement, not a question:
I am enough as I am right now, and if I don't buy this, I will still be enough.

Choosing to not buy something can be incredibly empowering. When I make the choice not to buy, I am essentially voting—for myself. I am deciding that I am enough as I am, and I don't need anything more to make me whole.

SIMPLIFYING MY WARDROBE

When I was a teenager, I loved to dress in kaleidoscopic, patterned Indian tops with beaded detail, paired with a thick floor-length chartreuse sweater jacket with ruffled edges and cuffs. I wore my chestnut hair in wacky bouncing dreads. When I experienced manic episodes in my early twenties, I had a fetish for pairing fuchsia with tangerine, squeezing into snug, low-cut jeans and nearly painted-on tops, and wearing lime green chandelier earrings or large silver hoops.

The flustered morning conundrum of getting dressed would leave me frantic, overwhelmed, and fretting whether I had chosen the right outfit. I'd lose track of time playing dress-up, which usually resulted in missing breakfast and being late out the door. I would undergo a costume change at midday, sometimes twice a day if I could. I had piles of clothes in a rainbow of fabrics and costumes in colors that belonged in a circus clown's trunk. The world shimmered and shone, and I did too. I was living the full expression of "me" and loving it. But, after I began treating my bipolar disorder, something interesting happened. My technicolor wardrobe felt too stimulating, too destabilizing. What had once been a joyful expression of a creative personality bothered me, and the Ferris wheel of colors and patterns upset me. I needed to get away from the loud reminders of being unwell.

My inner artist wasn't being robbed of her creative expression. Instead, with treatment and increased stability, my life was being transformed from the inside out. I started to develop a preference for a classic palette of serene neutrals. The color and excess I once loved to get lost in overwhelmed me and recreated sensations of being out of control. I yearned for less, and room to heal.

I read about the uniform dressing habits of leaders such as Steve Jobs, who simplify their wardrobe to reduce the decisions they need to make each morning. This helps avoid decision fatigue later in the day and conserves energy for the projects that matter the most. I remembered my love for my orchestral black uniform that made me feel like a true professional. And so I worked to replace my technicolor clothing, paring down to a minimalist, classic neutral wardrobe, one timeless, high-quality piece at a time. I chose articles that look modern and professional, and above all, are comfortable!

My current wardrobe is simple and uncluttered, which streamlines the daily process of getting dressed. Every outfit makes me feel great, and everything coordinates due to a limited palette of mostly black, charcoal, navy, and a little royal blue and dark red. I still love color, but now I accent with a small, classic accessory instead of wearing a rainbow.

Musicians wear black for most performances, so when I wear black I feel classy, professional and put together. Like other neutrals, black is spacious; it makes room for big ideas and concepts and allows both me and my audiences to focus on the music when I perform alone or with others.

Here are some tips for simplifying your wardrobe:

- **Embrace purging your closet.**

Try on everything you own and give away anything that doesn't look or feel fantastic *now*. Clothes that don't fit or that you don't wear are just taking up space and energy.

- **Keep quality, but not if you don't wear it.**

I've fallen into this trap before, feeling like I need to keep something because it is "good quality" or something I spent significant money on but never wear. Try to sell or consign it if you can't bear giving it away.

- **Don't keep an item just for the memories.**

That is what photos are for! The new you needs room to thrive. I had fun giving away some early '00's kaleidoscopic pieces to my teen cousin who loves them! Also, let go of pieces you never wear but hang onto because someone special gave them to you and you feel the need to honor them. The message has been received: they love you! Now you can let the piece go.

- **Less and simple is more.**

Recognize that you only need about a week or two's worth of basics. Everything else is clutter. Enjoy owning just a few classic pieces that go with everything. You don't need multiple items in certain categories. For example, you probably don't need four black blazers. Keep *one* quality piece in each category. (I am, however, guilty of keeping too many black t-shirts!)

- **Try the "better or different" rule.**

Don't keep an item unless it is "better or different" than what you have, and if you identify a better item that serves the same purpose, donate the other one! Think "one in, one out!"

- **Lose the uncomfortable stuff.**

Throw out any underwear, socks or t-shirts that are uncomfortable or have holes. If you intend to mend anything, do it now or throw it out. Give t-shirts and socks a new life as handy household rags.

- **Give yourself room to breathe.**

Enjoy the reduced clutter of owning just a few, classic, quality items that go with absolutely everything!

KEEPING MY HOME

I used to apply the "more is more" rule to my home too, and thought I needed to display every item I owned. My personal space always had a frantic, chaotic vibe that replicated my inner life. But, as with my wardrobe, I came to dislike my disordered, over-stimulating living space, and over time I adopted a more minimalist approach that helps my home feel relaxed, spacious and centered.

My living space is now simple and tidy, mostly white, off-white and gray, accented by a cheerful cushion or two. I also have a gallery wall of pictures and art and a wall of fun wallpaper, and I rotate my paintings on our brick wall. An uncluttered space doesn't have to be sterile. My studio and bedroom walls, bookshelf, reading chair, bedspread, and cello case are eggshell colored, which, for me, evokes peacefulness and clarity. I keep my studio feeling spacious and open for learning with minimal furnishings, and I keep my teaching supplies organized in pretty vintage bowls and neutral-colored felt baskets I made myself. Now I am very selective about my home and my personal space. I only display posters and pieces of art that are linked to positive memories and items that connect me with nature and inspire creativity. For instance, a wooden Buddha bowing in prayer reminds me to look inward and connects me to the present moment. While it might not be easy or even possible to keep your home feeling uncluttered and serene if you live with children or other people, even a small gesture like clearing a table, shelf, or drawer can make a big difference to how you feel.

I also exhibit a small selection of photographs of family and friends. This includes some wedding photos which remind me of one of the happiest days of my life, just before I learned that I had a mental illness. I display visual images that mean something to me—my own paintings to remind me of my love of art, and drawings made by my cello students to remind me of my love of music and teaching—and things that represent professional or academic accomplishments, such as posters and ads from memorable concerts and university and graduate school diplomas. Try simply swapping two photos or pieces of art to change the feel of your space and lift your spirits.

On a shelf in my studio, I keep two pairs of smooth, round stones. I found one pair—near-circular gray discs—within seconds of one another on a pebble beach in Nova Scotia. My spouse found the others—white, pebbly spheres—in British Columbia. The stones remind me of the wonderful trips they came from. A few plants—jade, succulents, a peace lily, and snake plant—connect me with nature, inspire creativity, and clean the air. These personal touches tell my story and make for an inviting space that feels like home.

THE INTERNET AND SOCIAL MEDIA

The internet is an essential part of our lives, and social media is an irresistible daily fixture that distracts us unceasingly. Every minute, Facebook users "like" more than four million posts, and over 300 hours of new video is uploaded to YouTube[25]. While surfing the web used to be a stationary activity done from desktop computers, now smartphones let us disappear down the online wormhole any time, any place, and on any occasion—during meetings, at the dinner table with our families, and while "visiting" friends in person. Half of our day is now spent consuming media on personal electronic devices, and the average person checks their smartphone 80 times a day. Eighty times. That's roughly once every 12 minutes[26].

In the '90's when email was first adopted, it was a much slower form of communication that could only be checked sporadically. It required a desktop computer and a dial-up internet connection. Now, however, most people are alerted immediately to new messages, and instantaneous responses are expected. Also, more people are beginning to favor the even quicker and more concise nature of text or instant messaging.

All of this hyper connectivity, speed, and constant stimulation concerns me. Studies are showing that the more time we spend on the internet or social media, the more likely we are to suffer from mental health issues. The potential addictiveness of social media has been compared to alcohol, cigarettes, and certain drugs, all of which cause the release of similar chemicals in our brains. Social media is a common 21st century phenomenon for healthy people, but for a person with a mental illness, its influence is magnified. It has a sneaky way of making you feel sad, depressed, or inadequate when all you see are perfect posts about happiness and successes, and if care isn't taken, it can prompt mood swings. If I'm experiencing depression, for instance, social media can easily feed that depression by showing me what everyone else is doing and what I'm not doing. I get pulled off center and I make unwholesome and unhelpful comparisons.

I was particularly vulnerable when I used to let myself check social media upon waking. My precious first thoughts would be, *good morning! Look at what everyone else is doing!* I also used to scroll incessantly just before going to sleep, directing my last thoughts of the day to unnecessary things like wondering if I should be learning to play Bluegrass music, traveling to Bali, or having babies, because that's what everyone else appeared to be doing! It was easy to forget that I was being bombarded by curated highlights of people's lives, glimpses that give the illusion that others experience perfect, exciting careers, endless delight in their children, or Instagram-worthy meals every day. On top of FOMO, I fretted about taking a step back, socially. What if I missed out on hearing about an amazing concert, learning about a gig opportunity on social media, or knowing what my friends and colleagues were up to? Only gradually did I realize that the effects on my mood were not worth the tradeoff, and it was much healthier to focus on and savor *my* life.

The expectation of an instantaneous response to electronic communications also put pressure on me as a freelance musician. Knowing that my next job could be in my inbox at any second meant I was constantly looking at my phone, anxious for the next opportunity. I sometimes receive gig emails that are copied to many other cellists and end with "The first person to reply gets the gig!" With a pounding heart, I used to race to reply, desperate to "win." And if confirmation didn't arrive, thoughts of inadequacy would distract me and sometimes result in sleeplessness. Now, I ask myself if I actually want to do a job that finds candidates this way, and remind myself that if I don't get it, *it wasn't meant for me!* Also, is the way it makes me feel really worth it?

And then there's the issue of over-stimulation (which I try to minimize) and distraction (which impacts my time management and ability to focus). When we interact with screens, our nervous systems shift into fight-or-flight mode, causing us to feel overstimulated and "revved up[27]." This constant stimulation has ill effects on our mental and physical wellbeing, because it impairs our ability to regulate our mood, attention, or energy according to our environment.

Out of necessity I have developed a strategy to monitor and manage the constant stimulation and hyperconnectivity of email,

153

texts, and social media. I can't afford such unregulated access because, for me, the costs of exposure outweigh the rewards. So, my rule of thumb is a minimalist one: when it comes to electronic communication, less is more.

I have found that I enjoy greater wellbeing when I am a little distanced from social media. I used to ensure this by not having the apps installed on my phone, but now that I have developed the habit, I can abstain without being tempted. I still enjoy participating in social media, especially making the occasional post when something really fun or significant occurs in my life. But checking several times a day or repeatedly scrolling to see what friends and family are up to actually makes me feel unhappier, and distracts me from the richness of my real life. To keep a healthy distance, I might only check email during business hours and social media once or twice a day, briefly, on a break between teaching or rehearsing, or a short check-in at the end of the day before my wind-down routine. Aside from the odd post containing an exciting update or announcement, I usually find that I have missed *nothing*. For text messaging, I try to use it for short communication only, like letting someone know I'm on my way, asking for grocery requests, or as a tool to set up a meeting, coffee, or phone date in person. If someone tries to engage deeply, I'll suggest a time for a phone call or video chat.

With all that said, I also recognize how fortunate we are to be living at a time when we have access to virtually any piece of information, all in the palm of our hand. The internet and social media bring some significant benefits to the realm of mental health, too. People are talking about mental illness more than ever, and electronic communications can advance and amplify the discussion. A growing number of wellness organizations also post on social media and provide other forms of public education and advice. It's now possible to find like-minded online friends who are self-aware, open, and who may also be treating a mental illness. Connecting with others can be comforting, can help you gain confidence, and lets you exchange tips and tricks.

Social media helps bring people together and develops stronger support networks. There are many mental health support groups available through Facebook, including specific groups for every type of mental illness from depression and anxiety, to bipolar disorder and schizophrenia. There are even subgroups for specific religious and LGBTQ mental health communities. Online forums are another useful resource. For example, *BP Magazine* offers an online support forum for anyone affected by bipolar, including friends and family, at bphope.com.

So, provided we develop and maintain appropriate boundaries, the electronic world has advantages for those of us with a mood disorder. We just need to make sure that electronic communication serves us and not vice versa. We need to safeguard our mental health and stay centered.

A wonderful part of my work as a musician and educator is that I *have* to be physically present and mentally focused to do my job well. I can't play the cello while I'm on my phone or computer. My acoustic instrument is a low-tech refuge from the deluge of digital: I sit down with my stringed maple and spruce box and horsehair-strung Pernambuco bow. I read from paper and write in pencil. When I teach I am with my students and *their* stringed wooden box, present and listening, face to face, cello to cello. When I'm playing with an ensemble, I am totally immersed in realizing sound from the notes on the page in front of me and connecting with my colleagues. I have found that the more attention I focus on my work, the less interest I have in what's happening on social media, which is a nice side effect. I do, however, enjoy sharing gig posts!

My partner does not have any social media accounts, which has been enormously helpful with my decision to take a step back from social media, and because we don't communicate in a virtual world other than texting when necessary, our relationship feels strong, present, and real. While I sometimes wonder if it would be fun to connect publicly over social media like some people seem to enjoy, posting the occasional couples' photo feels like enough.

This has helped me stay grounded, avoids miscommunication with my spouse, reminds me that my relationship is happening in real time, and keeps me present and focused on our real life.

LIVING MINDFULLY

Mindfulness—the mental state that we achieve when we focus our awareness on the present moment—has been an important aspect of my life for many years. It alleviates stress, anxiety, depression, and ruminating and destructive thoughts. Music first connected me to mindfulness long before my diagnosis, because playing music brings me into the present moment like nothing else. I play my best when I think only of the music and the sound I am creating and enter a state of flow, a condition where I am fully absorbed in the activity. I connect deeply to every note and listen to how the sound of my colleagues' instruments merge with mine, and I am absorbed and transported. Playing my cello softens the critical voices inside me and clears my mind of distractions. I control the bow to create the exact sound I want and listen intently to the length, shape, and tone of every note. I feel the strings under my fingers and my cello resting on my body with my knees hugging it. Playing well requires so much focus moment by moment, making it a great way to practice mindfulness.

I also connect with mindfulness through yoga, which means "union." (More about yoga in Chapter 7.) The central focus of yoga is not the body or the soul; it is the mind. You don't have to do poses or fold yourself into a pretzel to practice union through yoga. You can do it simply by being present and by connecting to what it is, here and now. No matter what is going on in my life or what kind of day I am having, when I'm on my yoga mat, I am there and only there.

When I first started attending yoga classes, my mind would race with self-conscious thoughts as I waited for instruction to begin. I would wonder about others, worry about where my mat was, and fret about bumping into anyone else or grazing a limb, all while thinking about what else was going on in my life! But these distractions passed once the class started. As we began to breathe in unison, I would feel each breath filling my lungs and reaching every one of my internal organs. Each new breath took me from the crown of my head down to my toes. I would notice spaces in my body that felt tight from sitting and playing my cello or that were surprisingly flexible. Every changing posture created awareness of the present moment.

Through yoga I learned to acknowledge and embrace discomfort, rather than resist it. I became connected with my whole self, exactly as I am. Realizing the benefits of this practice, I gradually translated the mindfulness of my yoga practice to other parts of my life and, as with music, embraced mindfulness as a regular practice. Instead of chasing negative thought patterns or wondering how I measured up to others, I eased my worry by bringing my attention to my breath, noticing the present moment, and reminding myself that the present is really all that we have. Without yet knowing I had bipolar disorder, I was already applying the healing practice of mindfulness, and later this daily discipline helped me accept my diagnosis.

Being alone in nature is a great place to begin experiencing mindfulness, and I especially like to practice near water, which is an incredible tool for developing awareness. When I am near a lake or the ocean, I love gazing at the changing surface, noticing the reflection of the sky, and imagining how the water sustains the life below. I also use water in smaller ways to trigger mindfulness. Upon waking, I drink a glass of water and turn my attention to the temperature and texture as it refreshes and hydrates my cells. When I make tea, I take a few deep breaths while waiting for the water to boil, or I look out the window and appreciate the day. On an afternoon break, tea (decaf or herbal) helps me reconnect and relax before my next work activity.

When I care for my plants, I notice their green leaves and fresh smell. I think about how they purify the air and I am aware of nourishing another living being. And when warm water pours over me in the shower, I clear my mind by imagining the water washing away thoughts or feelings such as frustration, stress, anger, or fear. Taking a hot bath before bed has, for years, been one of my favorite ways to de-stress.

Caring for another living creature can also take you outside yourself and keep you grounded and mindful in the present moment. Research has shown that petting a friendly dog lowers blood pressure, slows the pulse, regulates breathing, relaxes tense muscles, and reduces the release of stress hormones[28]. I have loved and enjoyed the company of animals most of my life. I grew up with a family dog, lovebirds, pocket pets, and rabbits, and in middle school I volunteered at a pet store on weekends.

There are even therapy dogs and other animals who are specially trained to support those who suffer from depression, anxiety, bipolar disorder, and PTSD. Recently I was performing in an orchestra concert in my home town and visited a cat café on a night off with my parents. There, patrons enjoy coffee in a room filled with friendly cats, which are there for you to pet, watch, and play with. I was amazed at how fun and relaxing it was to visit with them. The cats benefit from the human company and are available for adoption, and the café helps them find permanent homes.

My long-time pet was a black lionhead dwarf rabbit named Weenie, who lived to be 10 years old. He was litter-box trained and roamed free when I wasn't teaching. He was great company and hilarious. I would feel his soft fur when I petted him and he would lean in to enjoy the attention. Watching "The Ween Machine" hop around or giving him something to nibble brought me into the present moment, and even when I was feeling unwell and incapable of doing anything else, taking care of my rabbit connected me with another living being and reminded me that I was needed. Weenie always cheered me up and gave me and my spouse a lot of laughs, including singing his "theme songs." When Weenie eventually "crossed the rainbow bridge," we decided to remain pet-free, but I continue to connect mindfully with animals by visiting friends' pets and enjoying the cats and dogs of the neighborhood.

MAGICAL ROCKS? ON KEEPING A TALISMAN

Yes, rocks! Hear me out!

For as long as I can remember, I have been fascinated by everything about rocks, minerals, and gemstones—their age, beauty, the stories they could tell, not to mention the incredible series of events that led to their formation. No wonder magical properties have been attributed to stones for millennia. They are color and magnificence, born of heat, pressure, and hardship. They are weathered by the elements but resistant at the core. Rocks have seen it all.

I keep rocks as talismans: a polished rose quartz, peach selenite, smooth, round river stones, and, as recommended by a friend, a polished lapis lazuli and orange calcite. Karin Porter describes a talisman as a special object that is thought to have magical properties and brings good luck[29]. It's kept at hand for comfort and protection. A talisman can be something that you choose yourself or a gift from a friend, family member, or therapist. Or perhaps the right talisman chooses you! However you obtain it, a talisman is an object that you feel connected to and that stirs positive emotions.

My polished rose quartz fits perfectly in the palm of my hand. I picked it out with my spouse, who bought it for me when I was having a very hard time. It represents for me the qualities of self-love and acceptance. My peach selenite is similarly sized and I keep it for mental clarity, transformation, and protection. I sleep with these rocks on my nightstand or sometimes under my pillow. Sometimes I'll slip one into my coat pocket to hold when I need strength and comfort.

It is also pleasing and satisfying to find a perfect, round, polished river rock. I relate to what they had to go through to take on their shape, an arduous experience that makes them perfect exactly as they are. I am very drawn to smooth rocks that are circular, oval or egg-shaped, and I keep one in my purse. It's nice to touch and helps me feel centered.

When I was a child, a favorite place to occasionally spend pocket money was the gem store. The mother and daughter who worked there were full of mystery. They had long red tresses, wore necklaces, and adorned their fingers with large silver rings mounted with polished minerals. My brother and I were engrossed with the baskets of polished rainbow gems, crystals, and mystical "break your own" geodes that cost a dollar. We would choose a stone to buy or, better yet, wait for the right stone to choose us, one that felt just right.

I find rocks awe-inspiring. They have the ability to lift me out of my own struggles and give me perspective. I think about how they came to be, their ancient history, and how they will continue to exist when our lives are long past.

CHAPTER 6

The Value of Dedicated Listeners

At different times in my life, I have had the benefit of working with a "dedicated listener," a professional who worked with me one-on-one and whose job it was to listen to me and help me address an emotional, psychological, or behavioral issue that was troubling me. There are many different kinds of such listeners including psychiatrists, psychotherapists, psychologists, counsellors, social workers, and life coaches, and sometimes the work of these practitioners overlaps. The dedicated listener that is more familiar to me is the psychotherapist, and the process, psychotherapy, is intended to relieve whatever symptoms I'm concerned about, help me change my behavior, help me cope with my illness, improve the way I function, and give me insights that help me grow as a person.

PSYCHOTHERAPY: ONE-ON-ONE HELP

My first experiences with psychotherapy precede my diagnosis of bipolar disorder. When I was a teenager I saw a family counsellor while experiencing severe depression and suicidal thoughts following a pregnancy scare and other stress at home. The counsellor made sense of my terrifying thoughts, feelings, perseverating (the inability to let something go) and confusion, and gave me tools to help me cope and learn from my experience. It was my first time really opening up, and I couldn't believe how much better I felt after talking to someone, especially someone who could offer a completely safe, judgement-free environment. After my first session I felt physically lighter when I left the office! That's how I knew that talking to a dedicated professional listener was really effective for me.

Later, when I was struggling in university, I sought treatment at the student services health center. Following a break-up with my high school sweetheart, I was in such a crisis that I missed two university exams. The counsellor helped me see my feelings of loss and distress as a normal and natural response to a break-up. She encouraged me to safe-proof my apartment and had me sign a contract with her, stating that I wouldn't follow through with harming myself or ending my life. I felt that someone cared about me, and in making me feel accountable to another person and to myself, the contract helped me work through the situation.

One summer years later, when I was in a cello master class program at the Banff Centre, I made appointments with an on-site therapist to help me work through performance anxiety and the depressive crashes I experienced when I didn't play my best. It didn't matter to me that I didn't know the practitioner well—in some ways, it was even easier to open up to a complete stranger. I just needed to talk to someone, and I knew that whomever it was, their job would be to listen and help. I gave the therapist a detailed family history and outlined my early life traumas and stressors. I shared my feelings of inadequacy and the despair I sometimes felt after a master class performance. The therapist was able to make connections between the early childhood challenges I faced—and how they related to the way I experienced my life events now—and the confidence struggles I faced as a musician.

Up to that point, the anguish I experienced about my musical performances had been my own secret. But when it was heard by the on-site therapist at the Banff Centre and aired out to dry, it became valid and real. I started to see things objectively, which helped me feel less alone, and I started to feel optimistic, as if something inside had healed. I could see how far I had come and how hard I had worked. I left with a sense of self-efficacy and a new confidence in my playing and in myself.

I went on to find a psychotherapist at the Artist's Health Centre in Toronto, where I could see someone on an artist's subsidy. When that ran out, I was referred to the Centre for Training in Psychotherapy, where I was interviewed and paired with a student therapist at a reduced rate. That was how I found my current therapist, whom I have been seeing for several years.

After I was diagnosed with bipolar disorder, psychotherapy took on a new significance. My therapist, along with my psychiatrist, helped me to understand and accept my bipolar disorder by exploring the feelings I had about my diagnosis. Through psychotherapy I accepted my illness as being a part of *me*, but not all of me. I came to understand my past experiences and behaviors, to rewire my destructive thought patterns, and to develop strategies for coping with stress. As a result, I became committed to my recovery, and I can now enjoy my life to the fullest.

I have noticed that the improvements in my life from undergoing psychotherapy—as well as reading related books alongside—have had a ripple effect. For example, my spouse has absorbed, by osmosis, my insights, communication techniques, and coping strategies, which have in turn improved his own life and wellbeing, as well as our relationship. I am also able to share my insights with friends, family members, my bipolar meetup group, and my readers, which helps inform and empower us all while destigmatizing mental illness. My students also benefit from my improved intuition and communication skills, the deep sense of empathy I have developed through practice, and my extensive experience in dealing with the frustration and the emotional challenges involved in learning to play the cello.

Relationship benefits are only some of the paybacks of the process. Psychotherapy has also taught me basic psychological concepts and life skills that I routinely apply in my daily life. When I can put a name to something—even on a temporary or experimental basis—and notice what is really going on inside me and others, I am better able to adapt or respond to what's going on. In turn, that helps me remain intact and stay strong.

Of the many things I have discovered in psychotherapy and through my reading, four things stand out the most: the ability to assert my personal needs and boundaries, the importance of speaking my truth, the concept of projection, and the practice of active listening. These four things contribute to the stable inner and outer lives that I treasure.

MY WHITE PICKET FENCE: PERSONAL BOUNDARIES

The first key thing that I have learned through psychotherapy is how to identify, establish, assert and validate my personal needs and boundaries. Even in the years before my diagnosis, I found it impossible to speak up around my personal needs, even on a basic level. I even *prided* myself in happily bending over backward to accommodate others. As I gradually began to get a handle on identifying and establishing my personal needs and boundaries as a whole person, my mental illness diagnosis called for a lifestyle makeover. This came with a brand-new expanded laundry list of new personal needs and boundaries that I never had before. With my rigorous new self-care habits and needs around them, I was determined to master the necessary skills to communicate my boundaries to others.

The first challenge was knowing what my needs were, and for this purpose it helped to make lists for myself. The bedtime and sleep routine in my holistic approach to daily life is one such list that I developed over time with trial and error. Once my routine, needs, and boundaries became clear to me I had to protect them, so I discussed different scenarios with my psychotherapist as they came up. I noticed that when I feel well, I can easily forget that my underlying condition needs consistent care and attention. I think of this forgetfulness as slipping into a "pre-diagnosis mode," that carefree feeling and way of being I used to have before I learned that I had a mental illness. Psychotherapy eased the yearning to feel "normal" and helped me accept the consequences of forgetting to manage my needs and self-care. I now know that communicating my needs, even when I am feeling well, is a skill I must practice if I am to maintain my wellbeing. Here are some tips I use for making sure I don't miss the opportunity to stay well in the moment and to help me communicate my needs to others:

- **I remember my limit.**

I remind myself of my boundaries and limits in advance, say before heading out to an event. I will state my need out loud to myself, and to those who support me: "We will leave by 9:30 pm," or "I'm just having soda with lime tonight."

- **I'll set an alarm reminder on my phone.**

This reminds me to leave or take my medication on time. In the beginning before my new habits were established, I would even set up reminders to avoid the bar, or stick to foods that support my nutritional needs.

- **I recognize my cues, and notice.**

Established habits have an action trigger or cue. For example, brushing my teeth is the cue to remind me to floss. Another cue might be when the server takes a drink order; that's my cue to say, "Club soda with lime." Or, when everyone leaves to go dancing after dinner, that's my cue to say, "I'm turning in." Noticing cues, just like triggers, is your moment to say what you need, instead of defaulting to the crowd's agenda.

- **I say what I need.**

I remember that no one really minds if I say out loud what I need, and I don't need be afraid. I don't have to ask for permission. Like most things for me, this took practice. Remember that other people will respect your wishes most of the time, especially if you use a confident, clear tone. If the friend, family member, or person serving you continues to push, simply repeat your statement, calmly and firmly.

- **I remember some helpful phrases.**

I developed a repertoire of phrases that clearly convey what I need, for instance, phrases that help me pry myself away from events to get home on time, or phrases that help me say no to a second drink.

Here are some suggested phrases to help you say what you need:

- For exiting an email or text conversation: I'm now signing off for the night. Goodnight!
- I'd appreciate leaving earlier, if possible.
- I don't really drink anymore, thanks.
- I'll be able to start thinking about this project after next Tuesday.
- I'll be right back, I just need a minute.
- I'm fine with water, thanks.
- I hate to be a party pooper, but we need to head out in an hour.
- I'm off Tuesdays, but why don't we meet Wednesday?
- Just a head's up, I could use a rest stop in the next 20 minutes.
- Just one glass for me, thank you.
- Please get started, and I'll be there in a moment.
- Sounds great, but I'm afraid I'll have to miss this one.
- Thanks for a great evening, but I need to turn in.
- This was an awesome party. I hate to leave, but I have an early morning tomorrow!
- The morning won't work for me, but we can meet in the afternoon.
- We can only stay 'til __ o'clock, but thanks for the invite!

TRUTH AND HONESTY

The second important thing I discovered through psychotherapy is the importance of speaking my truth and the power of living honestly. But before I could appreciate truth, I had to face the reality of lies.

When we humans make mistakes, our brains come up with lies to protect us from any pain associated with the truth. We may do this innocently or without awareness. We tell small-scale fibs or white lies such as "I thought I sent you an email, didn't you get it?" These fibs help preserve our image of ourselves as "good" or "perfect," especially in the eyes of friends, bosses, coworkers, and loved ones such as parents or children. We also tell falsehoods because of the shame so many of us carry around admitting that we were in the wrong.

I used to tell seemingly harmless lies, until I realized that lying exhausted me. It took energy to remember what I had told so-and-so. Then, to save myself the embarrassment of being found out, it took energy to keep up with the story I had invented. I constantly maintained, pruned, and put effort into my falsehoods, and that was fatiguing.

One day, I had a flashback: the day my grandmother looked deeply into my eyes and repeated what she used to tell me as a child. "My darling, *always* tell the truth," she said. Valuable advice, but I'd really only applied it to the big lies: intricate, fabricated whoppers and classic storybook tall tales that I never bothered to put the effort into. Could my grandmother have meant something else?

As an experiment, I decided to apply my grandmother's advice to little things, white lies like "I didn't get that email," that I told to maintain my perfect exterior. What, I asked myself, was the worst thing that could happen if I owned up to an honest mistake? What did I really have to lose if I admitted, heaven forbid, an *error* and made myself more vulnerable? The answer was in the clichéd saying: the truth will set you free. And, just like Pinocchio, I could become truly real.

When I finally did connect with my truth, it was liberating. I had nothing to hide and no stories, details, or misleading tales to remember. I stood on solid ground where no one could contradict me or question my reality. My behavior shifted, too. "I didn't realize our appointment time had been changed" became "I should have been more careful in reading your updates." "I forgot" became "I'm sorry, I didn't think the task was important enough for me to give it my full attention at the time." I started taking responsibility for *all* of my actions. Gradually I even stopped making the errors I was fibbing about in the first place. The more honestly I answered, and the more I owned up right away, the more weight came off my chest and the stronger my character became. As an added benefit, I strengthened my empathy: every truth reminded me that I am a whole, flawed human being like everyone else, and yet am perfectly fine the way I am. I am not so fragile and perfect that I need to protect myself by hiding from the truth.

Fibbing and shifting blame might be a defense mechanism or a coping strategy, but it's costly. If you're tired of paying those costs and want to stand on firm ground, here are some points to keep in mind for connecting with *your* truth:

- **Take a breath.**

Before you answer someone, pause and ask yourself, "Am I about to share what *really* happened?"

- **Remember, it will set you free.**

Connect with yourself and remember that telling and owning the truth will mean risking being vulnerable. But after your truth is shared, no one can contradict you. You are truly free.

- **Others prefer honesty.**

You'll be surprised to know that most people respect and prefer honesty because it makes people trustworthy. You probably prefer honesty too. If someone you know admits to making a mistake, chances are you feel more connected to them, because they shared their humanity with you. You can appreciate their effort and willingness to be real with you.

- **You are brave.**

Remember that telling the truth means being vulnerable, and being vulnerable requires courage. Most people don't have the guts to be real, and telling a lie is the easier way out. A harmless fib may seem easy, but it weighs on your heart and costs you over time.

YOUR PROBLEM, NOT MINE!

The third unconscious habit I discovered through psychotherapy is called projection. Projection occurs when there is a quality or emotion that, for whatever reason, we don't accept about ourselves (it can occur with positive qualities, too), so we unconsciously attribute it to someone else[30]. For example, if we don't want to admit to ourselves that we are intolerant, we might "project" this quality on someone else, thereby shifting the blame to them so we don't have to acknowledge or take responsibility for the trait in ourselves. Projection allows us to claim innocence and conveniently avoid addressing our own negative traits and emotions.

Humans don't knowingly or deliberately engage in projection. It's something that happens on an unconscious level, as one of our primary ways of protecting ourselves. Psychotherapy, however, makes us aware of unconscious drivers like projection—and the underlying past trauma or source of the behavior—and helps us recognize and monitor or manage these drivers in our daily lives.

I didn't know about projection until I was 25. Had I known about it sooner, I might have been spared countless instances of emotional suffering in my early life when I projected—or was projected *on*—by the people in my life.

Several years ago I joined a friend and her yoga teacher / spiritual guru (who also happened to be a psychotherapist) on a week-long yoga retreat in Mexico. Our primary focus was practicing yoga, but we also met to discuss our journals and to explore our individual journeys and personal transformations. I didn't yet know that I had bipolar disorder, but I somehow sensed the need to take care of my mental health, so I was a devoted yogi and saw my own therapist regularly at that time. During the yoga retreat, a minor misunderstanding arose between my friend and me. The yoga teacher told me I was projecting, and I had no idea what that meant. When she explained it to me, I was perplexed at first, then I instantly understood.

As children, my brother and I regularly took part in piano recitals with students of various ages and levels. One performer, a girl, was everything I wasn't. She was perfect in every way, from her blonde ponytails, matching dress and confident grin, to her flawless performances. An advanced pianist, she also excelled in dance, and she was just slightly younger than me, which made things even worse. This girl drove me up the wall. Our piano teacher would often gush about her in front of me, which made me feel insecure. I interpreted our teacher's praise to mean that I was garbage. Naturally, I was envious. But where the projection came in was when I decided that the girl hated me! Whenever I took the stage with my mousy hair and uninspired sonatina, I imagined the girl's grin turning into a glare. I even suspected that she wanted me dead, and I lost a lot of sleep thinking about that. When I later heard that the girl had plans to take up the cello, I was devastated. That was the one thing I had that she didn't! Returning home from recitals in a deflated heap and bemoaning my nemesis, I would be scolded by my parents, who would remind me how wonderful and gorgeous she was— reminders that only twisted the knife.

This and other instances of childhood projection turned into years of emotional torture, painful misunderstandings, and missed opportunities for friendship. I even remember accusing high school boyfriends of being unfaithful, when in fact I had kissed someone else! I only wish that at the time someone had been able to gently explain what I was doing and help me build true confidence in myself.

Once I did learn about projection, I routinely found myself entangled in it. But with practice I would catch myself in the act, pause, and ask, "Am *I* the one who actually feels this way?" Once I realized what I was doing I could extend myself empathy and deal with my feelings right from their source.

Four years after my yoga retreat, I caught myself again in the act. Cello in tow, I was on a 1000 km bicycle tour of Nova Scotia and Ontario, performing contemporary opera from stop to stop. I was still grappling with being diagnosed with bipolar disorder and was terrified of anyone on tour finding out, worried that my colleagues would reject me. So I imposed these feelings onto a colleague who was irritating me in other ways, and punished her with passive-aggressive behavior and sarcasm. When she asked me directly if I was unhappy on tour or if there was anything she could do to help, I replied that nothing was bothering me. I stayed angry. Later on, as we cycled to our next stop and I tackled some steep hills, I had a revelation: *she* was not the problem. It was me who felt hurt and isolated about my bipolar condition, and I projected my feelings onto her to relieve myself. My problem was *me*! I cycled back, apologized for how I had behaved, and shared that I was struggling. The colleague accepted my explanation and appreciated my honesty, and a huge weight lifted off my chest. We then went on to form a good friendship.

EARS OPEN

The other lesson I learned on my yoga retreat with my friend and wise teacher was active listening—how to truly hear people when they speak. This is a skill that has since helped me in my personal relationships, my teaching, and my encounters with others who are struggling.

At one point on the retreat my student expressed a concern, and without really hearing or acknowledging her, I defensively butted in and explained that no, that's not what I meant to say at all. The yoga teacher who observed our exchange asked me to pause.

"*Hear* what she is saying," she said steadily.

But I repeated, exasperated, "No! What I *meant* was ..."

Again, the teacher stopped me. "Hear what she is saying."

She then encouraged me to follow these steps:

1. After someone tells you what they feel, pause.
2. Take a moment to *hear* what they just said. Listen actively. For me, this means mentally reviewing and repeating what was said, instead of jumping to a response.
3. Acknowledge that you heard the person. This could mean saying, "I hear what you are saying." Even if you didn't quite hear them the first time, responding with an acknowledgement forces you to take an extra moment to really absorb what the other person said.
4. Respond to what was said by repeating it back. Simply restate what was said, starting with "What I am hearing is ..." and acknowledge the person's need without your own interpretation. For example, if the other person said, "I don't want to be late," your response could be, "I'm hearing that being on time is really important to you."

The practice of active listening helps ensure that the other person feels fully heard, which diffuses defensiveness and allows you to proceed with solving the dispute. When I started really practicing active listening, I also engaged in deep further study of what the therapist described to me as "nonviolent communication" (NVC). I went on to read Marshall Rosenberg's *Nonviolent Communication* and learned that active listening is a technique that he endorses. In addition to active listening, in my reading about NVC a whole world of kinder, more effective, truer and more intimate empathy-based communication opened up to me. (More about NVC in Chapter 9.)

TIPS AND ADVICE FOR FINDING
THE RIGHT PSYCHOTHERAPIST

A psychotherapist is not a medical doctor, like a psychiatrist, and does not prescribe or monitor medication. Where I live, a psychotherapist is a licensed healthcare provider who is overseen by a regulatory body called the College of Registered Psychotherapists of Ontario. He or she is trained and accredited. Most of the psychotherapists I have worked with practice psychodynamic therapy (talk therapy), which uses the format of a conversational relationship to address problems associated with daily living. Many people who have a mental illness have also had traumatic experiences of abuse or painful loss. Through psychotherapy, we can help heal past trauma, make sense of living with a mental illness, and develop ways to live more congruently with who we are.

If you only see your doctor or psychiatrist for your medication needs, you might consider expanding the group of experts that help you by finding a psychotherapist who can serve as your dedicated listener. Psychotherapy cannot cure your mental illness, nor is it a substitute for medication, but medication and psychotherapy can be complementary forms of assistance. They certainly are for me.

Psychotherapy is covered by some health plans, but you can generally expect to pay out of pocket. If the fees are too much for your budget, consider spreading the costs out over time by attending every other week or even once a month. You can see a psychotherapist long term or short term, though I advocate seeing a psychotherapist regularly for the long term. That way, the practitioner will get to know you intimately and be able to make connections in your life as it unfolds in real time. If traveling to your therapist is a problem, some will offer video calls in the comfort of your own home. Establishing a working relationship also takes time. If you meet with a psychotherapist and don't feel you "click" right away, consider giving it a few months to see if it might just take some time to get to know one another.

Whether you have a mental illness or not, I can't recommend regular psychotherapy enough. The process lets you look deeper into your personal history and your day-to-day coping mechanisms. For the time you are with your therapist, your soul—your heart, your whole self—is supported by your therapist in a safe space, free of judgement, where you don't have to hold anything back. Your thoughts, processes and reactions are like the branches of a tree, and psychotherapy helps you cut away the ones that hold you back. After this pruning, over time new shoots will sprout and grow into stronger branches, and gradually things change. They change differently than if we were doing it alone because we need the dedicated listener for the back-and-forth reflection that occurs in the relationship.

Psychotherapy allows you to develop your integrity—an awareness of your character's effects on other people—and to be a separate person that follows an empowered path. Many like to call the process "doing the work." If you do your work, you are rewarded with knowledge, insight, and understanding that allow you to create more meaningful relationships with yourself and everyone else in your life. When you take care of yourself in this way, you also look after the people you care about.

SUPPORT GROUPS: MORE DEDICATED LISTENERS

Not all of the dedicated listeners in my life are accredited experts or professionals whose services I pay for. I also receive valuable and regular help from a collection of voluntary listeners who form a support group where members encourage, comfort, and advise each other based on our common experiences and concerns. As a member of this support group, I too serve as a dedicated listener for others.

I never thought I would need or even want to meet with a support group, but once the severity of my illness sank in, I felt like an island. It seemed that I was the only one in the world with these experiences. The symptoms of a mood disorder can be overwhelming, and in my case, they ranged from a tumultuous ride down dark trenches of debilitating depression at one end, to kaleidoscopic manias that flowered into psychosis at the other end, with everything in between: difficulty concentrating, impulsivity, uncontrollable and irritable outbursts, and warp-speed operating. Imagine the isolation created by these symptoms and consider how magnified they would be if you faced them alone. Now, imagine walking into a room where *everyone* experiences symptoms like yours. For me, the discovery that I wasn't alone was both a surprise and a relief.

Friends and family listened to me, of course, but they knew little if anything about bipolar disorder, and had no idea how to best support me. Turning to them wasn't always helpful, and I was often embarrassed that I had confided in them.

When I was first diagnosed, I was uninformed about my condition too. I didn't know the first thing about bipolar disorder or who to talk to. Fortunately, my psychiatrist gave me a sheet of resources that included some great books and suggested a few local support groups to get me started.

The first support group I attended was at the Mood Disorder Association of Ontario in Toronto. It was a weekly bipolar support group, led by a facilitator. The group's composition fascinated me. Members represented nearly every age, race, and gender. There were Caucasian teenage girls, retirement-age South Asian men, Black women, Hispanic men, and so on. Bipolar disorder affects so many people, regardless of age, race, occupation, or social position. When I listened to others relay their symptoms and experiences, I was left speechless by how perfectly my symptoms matched some of theirs. Clearly, I belonged. I was comforted by the fact that there were others out there just like me.

Initially, I tried a few groups to see which one would be the right match, and I decided that the best fit for me was the Toronto Bipolar Disorder Meetup Group. I learned about this group through the Mood Disorders Association of Ontario group, and was directed to the popular meetup.com social group website. This group meets every other Wednesday evening, and I find the size of the group and the format of our meetings particularly appealing. Each session there are members who come often, as well as new people who want to try it out. We start in a circle and introduce ourselves one by one, say a word about our diagnosis if we wish, and listen respectively to each other. Then the large circle breaks up into smaller groups, where we can listen and talk about any topic we wish. We can leave the conversation if it isn't serving us and no one takes it personally. Afterwards, there is an optional social at the nearby pub, with no pressure to drink alcohol.

This group has also helped me develop some good friendships. One of these friends is a vocalist that I worked with years ago. I remembered her mentioning, at the time, that she was bipolar. After I was diagnosed, I reached out to her, and we connected over coffee. When I told her about the support group, she had not yet found the courage to try one, so we started going to meetings together and have been supporting each other ever since.

A lot of valuable sharing takes place in the group regarding symptoms, medications, lifestyle, and other supportive care. One evening, a regular attendee mentioned he was having a hard time finding a psychiatrist. My own psychiatrist just happened to be accepting new patients, so I put them in touch and he has been receiving care ever since. Meeting in person with people who share your condition has an effect that no book or online resource can fully replicate. I especially found the group atmosphere comforting when I was a newbie. The other members listened to me with experienced ears, and I got to learn about other people's symptoms and to compare them with my own. I was assured that the side effects of my medication were common, and that my symptoms were perfectly aligned with the symptoms of bipolar disorder. I was no longer alone.

FINDING AND ATTENDING SUPPORT GROUPS

Whether you enjoy meeting new people or prefer to keep your cards close to your chest, a support group offers something for everyone. You don't need to have an official diagnosis to join many support groups, so these can be a great way to meet other people who share your symptoms, and your participation might help you get the diagnosis or treatment you need. If you are fairly sure that you experience symptoms of anxiety, for example, try joining a group for people who suffer from anxiety and see if it resonates with you. That said, this can lead to confusion for some people, so discuss symptoms with a doctor or psychiatrist first.

Here are some things I like to remember when I am thinking about whether or not to attend my support group:

- **I might be able to help someone else.**

On the days I don't feel like going (usually because I am feeling fine or I'm too busy or tired) I think about how I might be able to help someone *else* that night. Every time I remember this and end up going I'm glad I did, especially when I am able to help someone. Maybe you won't always need a group, but someone in the group might need you!

- **I don't need to contribute.**

You don't have to have anything eventful happening in your life to benefit from attending a meeting. You can just go as you are, and choose to not contribute if you don't wish to. Sometimes it's good to just go and listen.

- **I will feel better.**

It always brightens my day to greet the familiar faces at my support group. These acquaintances are an extremely important part of learning more about my illness and how to live with it.

- **It will strengthen my knowledge.**

In the beginning, I benefited greatly from the group. Now that I am more experienced with living with bipolar, I get a lot of fulfilment from educating and sharing my experiences with others. Helping others strengthens my knowledge and reminds me of how I can continue to keep taking care of myself. And, in turn, others pick up insights from me that help them live better, too. Remember what you have been through and that you have a great deal of insight to share with others.

JOURNALS: THE PORTABLE LISTENER

At times, when it is late at night or I am away from home, I need to talk to someone and get something off my chest—and I need to do it immediately. Long before I discovered the power of talking to a dedicated listener, I confided in my journal. A journal is available any time you need it, and writing in it can be a powerful and transformative practice. It certainly has been for me.

Sometimes I journal when something is deeply troubling me. Other times I journal simply to remind me of the wonderful day I had or to remember the details of a trip and list the things I am grateful for. In dark times, I can re-read these positive entries to remind me that better days are on the horizon. When it comes down to sorting out a dilemma, I find writing it out long-hand helps me process it, almost as if my problem is leaving my brain, traveling down my arm, through my pen and onto the paper. This also helps me with mindfulness, as the process of handwriting leaves me with more time to digest my thoughts and connect with the present.

I recommend buying a journal that you find beautiful and inspiring, in a large enough size so that you can write freely and easily. I also love a nice, inky pen that flows easily and doesn't smudge (especially important if you are a lefty, like me). And if I only have a smudgy pen, I keep a piece of folded scrap paper under my hand as I write. Keep your journal in a private place so you know you can completely let go without worrying that it will be read by anyone but you.

When I was taking summer master classes at the Banff Centre, I was reading Julia Cameron's *The Artist's Way*, with the hope of unlocking some areas where I felt stuck as an artist. One of the practices she recommends is "morning pages," which is writing an unedited stream of consciousness for 20 minutes or so upon waking in the morning. While I was no stranger to journaling, trying to purge my mind first thing in the morning seemed like an interesting way to make some discoveries.

When I wrote my morning free-falls, I was able to connect with so many interesting things. It helped me become more present. I wrote about how my sore muscles from practicing seemed to melt away in the Banff Hot Springs, how I noticed that the appearance of the mountains changed with the weather, and how I felt like I was in the Black Forest, where I lived as a little girl. I could feel my creative and emotional channels opening, and I felt alive with the possibility that something fantastic might happen soon.

Following a bout of depression and feeling hopeless, I used my journal to write a stream of consciousness to process big questions that would look back at me from the page.

*What kind of a cellist do I wish to be? I wish to be: Solid. Stable. Beautiful. Sonorous. Diverse. Versatile. Always listening. Always playing for **sound**. Always thinking about getting the best sound out. To be less vertical, more horizontal. To make space for my projects and ideas. How can I make more space? What is my voice? Why do I play the cello? I am here to climb. I am here to open, to emerge.*

CHAPTER 7

Complementary Treatments

While medication, routine, sleep, good nutrition, regular eating, movement, and psychotherapy are the pillars of my holistic plan, there are other complementary treatments that contribute to my health and wellbeing. By complementary, I mean treatments that can safely be offered alongside conventional evidence-based medicine and that are compatible with the other elements of my plan. A word of caution: the information provided here is for informational purposes only.

Here, now, are some of the complementary treatments that I use or have used. I incorporate them into my life on a daily, weekly, or occasional basis, but however often I make use of them, each contributes to my overall wellness.

MASSAGE

As a performer I have always been aware of the benefits of regular massage therapy, which can treat both acute and chronic issues. It relieves the pain and stiffness in my neck, shoulders, hips and hands, as well as tension and trigger points in my bow arm from playing. Massage also eases the effects on my lower body from sitting. Since my first massage in my twenties, I have also noticed the benefits to my mental health and overall wellbeing; by promoting relaxation, massage helps manage stress, and reducing stress is essential to treating any mental illness.

For my mental health, getting a massage is an excellent form of care that greatly reduces my stress and makes my body feel loved, cared for, and overall amazing! The effects can last for weeks. I prefer to go all-out for 90-minute massages because my entire body is treated, and the effects seem to last longer. Treat your body to regular "maintenance." If you can, get regular massages to avoid building up tension in your body.

If I don't have the time or resources to book regular massage treatments, I do self-massage, such as massaging my scalp while shampooing my hair or rubbing almond oil into my neck and shoulders while moisturizing my face. I also love taking the time to massage my hard-working hands and feet as I relax with a movie or favorite TV show.

Massage is a form of touch, and regular touch is important for humans. I'm talking about friendly, platonic, non-sexual touch. Research has shown that touch can communicate a range of emotions. Simple hugging can reduce levels of the stress hormone cortisol, and being touched releases the feel-good brain chemical oxytocin that helps bond people together and promotes a sense of wellbeing. Touch makes us feel cared for.

Some psychologists have been referring to our lack of touch as "touch hunger," defined as a lack of meaningful, non-sexual physical contact with another person. Ignoring our natural yearning for physical contact with others can have profound consequences. Those who are "touch hungry" are said to present with similar symptoms as clinical depression, appearing withdrawn and speaking with a monotonous voice. So, it stands to reason that people with clinical depression may suffer from touch hunger, and that massage may reduce their depressive symptoms.

Whether you are single or partnered, you may not be getting the touch you need, so seeking regular massages can be a great addition to your care and can play a role in maintaining mental health. Massaging certain areas can stimulate the vagus nerve, which connects the brain to important organs like the intestines, stomach, lungs and heart. This nerve is therefore a part of the systems that affect digestive function, breathing, and heart rate, all of which can have an impact on mental health.

If you decide to seek massage therapy, your therapist will be open to discussing any reservations you may have due to sensitivity or discomfort from traumatic experiences.

Massage therapy treatments feel terrific on their own, and going to my appointment is a fun outing that always boosts my mood. I get excited the moment I book an appointment online, and look forward to my treatment for weeks. I love making the trip special for myself, and enjoy the stroll and scenery on the way there. I also really enjoy catching up with my massage therapist. Getting to know your massage therapist can lead to a cordial "appetizer-sized" relationship—this is especially good, since they get to know you literally from head to toe! My massage therapist also suggests self-care tips after the treatment, like reminding me to drink lots of water and take it easy for the rest of the day.

NATUROPATHIC DOCTOR SUPPORT AND SUPPLEMENTS

Naturopathy integrates Western medical diagnostics, science, and natural therapies. It focuses on holistic treatment—treating the *entire person*—and seeks to treat the root cause of illness instead of just the symptoms.

Important: naturopathic medicine is not a replacement for traditional medicine, and naturopathic treatments are not a substitute for psychiatric medication prescribed by your psychiatrist or physician, who has expertise in treating mood disorder patients. A naturopath can suggest treatments that work *alongside* your meds, and your psychiatrist or physician may be prepared to support such treatments.

Naturopathic remedies are intended to be safe and effective drug-free treatment methods that may include diet and lifestyle suggestions as well as vitamins and nutritional supplements, injections, and herbal remedies. Naturopathy treats a wide variety of conditions and ailments, including cardiovascular and digestive issues, immune and skin problems, hormone imbalances, pain, mood disorders, and stress conditions.

In Ontario, naturopathic doctors are regulated healthcare providers who must meet the prescribed entry-to-practice standards and demonstrate the required knowledge, skill and judgement. They use an evidence-based approach and work hard to stay up-to-date on the latest scientific research. For instance, during my appointments my naturopath often checks an online database of the latest studies and scientific journals to support her treatment plan for me.

Appointments are conducted in a clinical setting and include in-depth physical examinations, as well as laboratory and diagnostic testing such as blood and saliva tests. If you seek complementary care for your mental health, a naturopath will examine you thoroughly and take note of your current diet, lifestyle, and stress levels, as well as the medications that you take. They will conduct any necessary tests and will recommend natural treatment options tailored to your needs.

I first started seeing my naturopath for my gastric reflux and stress, for which she recommended digestive enzymes and an adaptogen herb called *rhodiola rosea*. But when I learned that I had bipolar disorder, I wondered if there was anything additional she could do for my mental health. My naturopath took the time she needed to examine my medical history thoroughly— including my psychiatric care—and noted that I attend regular psychotherapy. She also asked detailed questions about my diet. For treatment alongside my psychiatric medication, she added a daily dose of myo-inositol, which is a naturally occurring pseudo-vitamin used to treat fertility and insulin resistance in women. It helps regulate signal transmission for neurotransmitters such as serotonin and hormones such as insulin, and has been shown to relieve symptoms of depression, anxiety, panic attacks, and OCD. In my case, myo-inositol helps in two ways: it treats my mood and it regulates my menstrual cycle, which is affected by an endocrine disorder called polycystic ovarian syndrome.

My naturopath also added a high-potency B complex vitamin and vitamin D. She emphasized the importance of eating foods rich in B vitamins and getting "smart" amounts of sun exposure, which is the easiest way to get vitamin D.

B vitamins such as B6 and B12 are associated with mood regulation and are known to have an energizing effect and contribute to a strong immune system. Deficiencies can result in depression, anxiety, and fatigue. Because the B vitamins work together, your naturopath may suggest a product that combines B vitamins in proper proportions, and for people with bipolar disorder, such a supplement can reduce anxiety, irritability, and premenstrual mood symptoms. My naturopath also offers vitamin B12 injections to combat depression or depressive symptoms of seasonal affective disorder. The injections are thought to have a stronger and longer-lasting effect as they bypass the gastrointestinal tract, but are not necessarily appropriate for people who are hypomanic, i.e. in an elevated mood state.

Vitamin D has also been shown to be effective in treating bipolar disorder and other mental illnesses. It is also the only vitamin that is a hormone, and it assists with the absorption of calcium as well as activating genes that regulate the immune system. It releases neurotransmitters such as dopamine and serotonin that affect brain function. Researchers have found vitamin D receptors on parts of the brain that are linked to depression[31].

In one study, adults who received high levels of vitamin D reported improvement in their depressive symptoms after two months of treatment[32], and many studies have shown similar results by treating vitamin D deficiencies through supplementation. While we are still learning about the connection between vitamin D and mental illness (and while there are still no concrete conclusions made), there is a strong correlation between groups who are at risk for vitamin D deficiency (such as adolescents, the elderly, obese individuals, and those with chronic illnesses like type 1 diabetes) and those who are at risk for depression. Low levels of vitamin D have also been reported in individuals with schizophrenia, and infants born in the winter months to mothers with depleted levels of vitamin D have been shown to have an increased risk of developing schizophrenia. People who experience seasonal affective disorder, with depressive symptoms during the darker months of the year, are often deficient in vitamin D. This deficiency is from lack of sun exposure and is more common in populations residing far from the equator. Many of us, even those who do not have a mental illness, are deficient in vitamin D due to poor diet and lack of sun exposure.

Vitamin supplements *alone* are not proven as effective treatment for mental illnesses like bipolar disorder, and any vitamin should only be taken under the supervision of your healthcare provider. Also keep in mind that the very best source of vitamins is real food. A nutrient-rich diet can go a long way to helping prevent and correct deficiencies, although a condition-related deficiency might make supplementation necessary.

When I'm feeling well, I like to check in with my naturopath at least once a year to make sure that I'm staying on the right course of my treatment plan.

YOGA AND MEDITATION

If you have a mental illness, practicing yoga can be an effective way to help manage your symptoms. I've been hooked since I first discovered its transformative power through that Rodney Yee VHS tape, and have pursued it consistently since then through classes at local gyms, practicing at university and neighborhood yoga centers, seeking classes while traveling, attending retreats in Mexico and the Berkshires, USA, attending small home-based classes, and now practicing at home with my current online subscription. Yoga is a low-risk, high-reward mindful activity to cope with stress, depression, anxiety, anger, irritability, and ruminating or destructive thoughts.

The word yoga means "union" in Sanskrit. Yoga centers around the connection between the mind and the body, and—when taught traditionally—yoga *is* meditation, a practice of becoming more aware of who we truly are. Yoga is based on the philosophy that we all have within us the components of happiness and peace, a place within where our true, unchanging nature exists. When we come back to that place, we restore our sense of wellbeing.

For my mental health, yoga has helped me develop my practice of mindfulness and a sense of self-acceptance. In classes, the teacher often draws attention to each of us arriving on our mats *exactly as we are*, which has had a powerful effect on me. As I discuss in the "Movement" section, connecting, moving, and focusing on your body is a powerful way to center the mind and take you out of your head. Practicing yoga has also strengthened my belief in practice in general, be it in yoga or in music. At first I used to avoid taking a yoga class because I had not practiced in a long while, but I have learned that I can always come back and always start again. This has given me the courage to return, no matter how long it has been.

Anyone can do yoga, regardless of age, size, flexibility or strength. If you currently practice, I encourage you to continue. And if you've never tried yoga, I urge you to give it a try. Classes are available in a wide variety of styles at different levels. Read the class descriptions at your nearby yoga or fitness studio and ask about which class would be most appropriate for you. Most studios offer beginner or introductory level classes, as well as slow-paced yin or restorative yoga classes that are suitable for all levels of experience. Trying a few different classes and teachers is also a good idea.

Most classes follow the format of a group session led by a trained and experienced teacher, but private instruction is also available. Yoga instructors have completed intensive teacher trainings and personal practice and, in my experience, are highly skilled and knowledgeable. They have studied the various styles and levels of physical postures that are practiced in yoga, breathing techniques, meditation and philosophy, as well as anatomy, physiology, and other subjects.

The only materials you need to bring are your yoga mat and comfortable clothes that you can move in. Any other props used in the class such as blocks, belts, or bolster cushions are usually provided by the studio. Be prepared to practice in a room shared with other people, unless you are taking a private class. I like to arrive early, so I can choose a comfortable spot for my mat and do some preliminary stretching, relaxing, or meditation. Bring an open mind and a willingness to pursue a new path to feeling better and connecting to your true potential. During the class, if a particular posture or activity is uncomfortable for you, you can simply lie down or wait for the instructor to introduce a more manageable variation.

If you wish to practice yoga in the comfort of your own home—or in addition to attending classes in person—you can subscribe to an online yoga studio. I have a subscription to online yoga classes, and they are a *terrific* way to keep up my practice. I can access nearly any type of class for almost any time duration—even as little as 10 minutes. I can search for classes that target a specific area of the body, like the neck or hips, or focus on meditation alone. When I can't decide, my online studio has a "surprise me" function, where you type in how much time you have and how you are feeling to find just the right class for the moment. As much as I enjoy the outing, social benefit, and personalized direction from a real live teacher, I love having the convenience of being able to practice in my own living room.

I also practice meditation on its own, and often spend the first 10–20 minutes of my day in quiet meditation, sitting with my eyes closed, and clearing my mind by noticing and accepting my thoughts without judgement. I set a timer and then focus on my breath. Sometimes I practice "square breathing," where I inhale for four slow counts, hold for four slow counts, exhale for four, then hold for four before repeating. The mindfulness I practice in my day-to-day life is also a form of meditation, and through mindfulness I am taking my meditation everywhere.

As I continue to use the skills and techniques I have discovered through yoga and meditation in my daily life, I experience a ripple effect that has brought me balance, coping strategies, awareness and peace. Yoga and meditation have empowered me to make space for what is important, have helped me let go of things from the past, and help me care for myself and live my life openly and truly.

AROMATHERAPY

Aromatherapy is the practice of using essential oils from plants to promote psychological and physical wellbeing. Our sense of smell is one of the strongest senses in terms of influencing brain activity. The olfactory system connects to the hypothalamus, the emotional processing and learning center of the brain, which is why smell can trigger strong memories. Essential oils are typically chosen for their scent, but aromatherapy isn't just about smelling pleasant scents. Different oils can provide different benefits to the user, depending on their properties. For example, lavender is famous for promoting relaxation and good sleep, and ylang ylang and chamomile can alleviate anxiety. Lemon and rosemary are great for lifting your mood, and peppermint (one of my favorites) stimulates and promotes mental clarity. Some oils, such as eucalyptus, have physical benefits such as relieving chest congestion, and tea tree oil is a natural antiseptic that can help treat acne-prone skin.

Although essential oils are a natural product, they are potent and need to be used carefully. Some, if applied directly to the skin, can cause irritation or an allergic reaction. When used correctly and safely, essential oils can enhance wellbeing and be an effective complementary treatment for a wide variety of symptoms.

I use essential oils in a room diffuser and have a travel kit of rollers for my neck, wrists, and temples. One of the oils in my travel kit is peppermint, which I find helps with focus, clarity, and decongestion when rolled around the neck as a "halo"— especially nice if I'm fighting a cold.

I also enjoy using essential oils–based natural solid perfumes from a favorite company that makes handmade self-care products, and I keep some in my purse and travel kit. While the scent is subtle, I love putting it on to encourage deep breathing, staying in the present moment, and overall mindfulness. This is especially useful while traveling and just before bed.

Aromatherapy emphasizes natural essential oils and not synthetic perfume or "fragrance oils," which are composed of synthetic chemicals and do not provide the same benefits as pure essential oils. However, if a synthetic product helps you feel great, then all the power to you!

Look for essential oils that come in opaque bottles, as clear bottles let in light, which damages the oils and affects their potency. Check the label to ensure that the essential oil is pure. You can find pure essential oils at many natural health food stores, specialty shops, some drug stores, and online.

You can also reap the benefits of aromatherapy by adding essential oils to natural cleaning products, skincare products, and cosmetics. Essential oils can be applied to the skin, but are extremely concentrated and should be diluted with a carrier oil, such as almond or grapeseed oil. You can also use the oils in compresses, for massage with a carrier oil, or in the bath.

If you share a workspace, you can use essential oils without disturbing other coworkers by dabbing a few drops on a cotton ball and inhaling the scent to boost your energy and mood or ease anxiety. If you have a private office, consider picking up an essential oil diffuser, which is an easy way to reap the benefits of the essential oil and change the atmosphere of a room. I use an essential oil diffuser in my teaching studio. The scent is subtle, but the effect is profound, and my students love it when the studio "smells like tea!"

You will want to research carefully the essential oil you are considering using and make sure it is compatible with you and any medication you are taking. You might also want to consider the extraction method that was used and to find out whether the plant crop was treated with pesticides.

Here are eight essential oils that I have experienced firsthand and that are known to be mood boosters:

- Bergamot (not to be confused with North American bee balm) is a citrus fruit used to flavor Earl Grey tea. It is used as a natural remedy for anxiety, for its stimulating and refreshing effect, and for evoking feelings of joy. Studies have shown that bergamot reduces symptoms of anxiety and depression and decreases blood pressure.
- Chamomile has soothing qualities that reduce stress and promote relaxation, and is often used as a natural remedy for general anxiety and for treatment of depression.
- Lavender is versatile and famous for its calming properties, which settle the nervous system, help reduce anxiety, combat depression and stress, and improve sleep. It's also used for treating headaches and migraines. Studies have shown that there are no adverse side effects to using lavender alongside medication to treat depression and anxiety.
- Lemon is a pick-me-up, and is also a great antifungal and antibacterial oil for using in natural cleaning products. I love mixing lemon with peppermint in my diffuser!
- Jasmine—like lavender—calms nerves, but is also used as an antidepressant, for enhancing self-esteem, and for evoking a sense of confidence.
- Peppermint is a great energy booster, invokes a feeling of mental clarity, and eases headaches. Studies have shown

that it can also help improve cognitive performance.

- Rosemary can be used to relieve muscle aches and pains, and has stimulating properties that combat mental fatigue and exhaustion and improve memory. Roman scholars used rosemary to improve memory while taking exams!

- Ylang ylang is used for enhancing self-confidence and mood and combating depression. It has a mild sedative effect, which can lower your stress response and help you relax. Inhaling the ylang ylang essential oil can have an immediate benefit in boosting mood and self-esteem. It is also said to help release negative emotions like anger.

Everyone from average consumers to medical professionals have experienced benefits from aromatherapy and reported a wide variety of responses. Like any complementary treatment, aromatherapy will be more effective for some people than others. It's important to try things and see what works for you.

CHAPTER 8

Work, Money, and Mental Wellness

I am a freelance musician. I don't have a standard job with regular hours, a boss, a salary, workplace benefits, or a pension. Instead, I support myself by weaving together different paid activities as they come along. Embarking on a career as a musician was a risky choice, and it seemed radical when I started out, but freelance careers are becoming more popular than ever, and now I feel like a seasoned participant in the "gig economy." I'm glad I chose this path and wouldn't want things any other way. Through hard work I now have a lifestyle that is both financially viable and artistically fulfilling. To get there, I had to develop healthy working habits, manage my money prudently, and maintain my minimalist values.

THE FREEDOM OF FREELANCING

As a self-employed musician, I perform as a solo and collaborative artist, a chamber musician, and an orchestral player. I am also a private music teacher. My workflow is variable, and my income, while currently steady, is not guaranteed. This might seem like a recipe for stress, but I have learned how to make my freelance career work for me in a way that supports my mental wellness.

The irony of freelancing is that the very things that make it amazing—working for yourself! doing what you love!—can compel you to make decisions that ultimately hurt you. When I began a full-time freelance career, I *thought* I had to make myself available at all hours, accommodate everyone else's schedules, and say yes to every opportunity. Working evenings and weekends is part of being a performer, but I used to deny myself *any* time off. I booked myself seven days a week at all times of the day, counting myself lucky to have so much work. Somewhere along the line I had got the idea that because I loved my work, it wasn't "legitimate," and I felt that I had to work twice as hard as the average person in order to compensate for this enjoyment. Friends and family with mainstream careers insisted that I take at least one day off per week, but I persevered. In my eyes, taking a day off was lazy and indulgent, and since my work was enjoyable, I didn't deserve it. My mindset was not only wrong and dangerous to my health, without knowing it, I was discrediting and stereotyping artists with my skewed view that loving your job meant you weren't really working.

It wasn't until I was faced with a serious illness that required treatment that I began to leverage my freelance flexibility to *support* my health, instead of using it as an excuse to work every hour, every day, with no boundaries. Knowing I had a mental illness to manage helped me develop a healthier work-life balance and to take my work seriously, no matter how much I enjoyed it.

I wish that it hadn't come down to a medical diagnosis to make me act, but it did. Since then, I've reevaluated my lifestyle and evolved a more balanced approach to making a living. My freelance career now supports my mental wellness in the following five ways. I hope that by sharing these self-care tips I help other self-employed artists or precariously employed people come up with a system that works for them.

1. I make sure to book at *least* one day off per week.

At first, this seemed impossible. Don't freelancers need to make themselves available to accept work at all hours when they can get it? Yes. But they also need time to regroup and refresh.

While I knew it wouldn't always be possible, a weekly goal of one day off seemed essential to managing my illness and reframing my work life. Most people have weekends, I reasoned. Why couldn't I try for one day? Being my own boss, I was the only one who could make it happen. Since my weekends are filled with teaching and concerts, I decided that, like many retailers, Monday would be my day off. This felt like a huge step, even extravagant. Who was I to think I deserved this? What about students who could only come on Mondays? But now I consider my day off as one way to put my health first.

Recently, I also shifted my teaching away from Friday because it's a popular gig day. I use my two personal days for me, not working for others. That might mean catching up on email, practicing, writing, exercising, personal appointments, visiting friends, or just recuperating.

As a freelancer, I feared that I would lose clients by taking days off, but I didn't. They adapted. Now, when students ask for a lesson time or when I book rehearsals, rather than asking, "What works best for you?" I offer a list of dates and times that suit me and simply do not offer Mondays or Fridays. Sometimes I have to compromise, but for the most part I get to keep my free days.

Realizing that I could create my own boundaries and didn't have to offer every cell of my being to clients and colleagues was incredibly empowering. If you don't respect your own boundaries, no one will.

2. I take advantage of my flexible work hours.

Although I can't control the timing of rehearsals and concerts, I generally set my own hours. When I have gigs I schedule lessons around them. When I know that a show will run late, I adjust my teaching schedule the next morning so that I get the rest I need. I also schedule 15-minute breaks in between lessons and appointments, so I can catch my breath and prepare for my next activity. Not rushing has made a big impact on my stress level!

Starting early simply doesn't work for me, nor is it conducive to the schedule of a working musician. So I decided that my earliest start time would be 10:00 am, which works nicely, and unless I have a late show I try to be in bed by 10:00 pm. I work hard, and working different hours doesn't mean I am "lazy." There are many ways to carve out a work day. Now, my work days are variable.

3. I can often work from home.

I am fortunate to be able to teach and rehearse at home in a bright, spacious studio. Many of my musician colleagues can't do that. They have to teach for music schools or rent studio space because playing music at home disturbs their neighbors or families.

When I wake up, my work is close at hand, and I don't have to worry about dragging a cello across town to teach! Working from home means I am available for deliveries, and can quickly change my clothes or go straight to bed when I need to. It also allows me to make healthy meals that support my nutrition plan. But it's easy to feel housebound, so at least once a day I take a walk around the block to refresh myself, and whenever I leave the house for gigs, I welcome the change of scenery.

4. I am able to choose projects carefully.

Early in my career, in order to get started, I had to accept a lot of work that was not artistically satisfying or financially rewarding, but was good experience. Now, however, I do not have to say yes to every project that comes my way. I am able to focus on work that is both artistically and financially fulfilling.

I get hired for a wide variety of projects, including performing and recording with many different groups. I play and teach within all genres of music, from Baroque and Classical to contemporary and pop. This diverse mix keeps things interesting, but to manage this variety I need to be skilled in time management so that I allocate the preparation time necessary for each project. Keeping a foolproof professional calendar helps me achieve this.

Over time, through effort, ambition, organization, and being easy to work with and good at what I do, I have developed an excellent reputation and created a reliable freelance career with steady income. I am doing work that I love, in an industry that I believe in, which brings me satisfaction and wellbeing.

5. I get to share my passion.

Sharing my love for the cello with students and making music with others is powerful and gratifying. I am fortunate and privileged to be able to combine these activities as a way to earn my living.

My skills as a performer feed my teaching, and my teaching strengthens my technical and musical ability. The more experience and knowledge I accumulate as a cellist, the more I can give. My students improve every year, and the positive feedback I receive from them boosts my spirits and brings me joy.

Through teaching, I have also developed heartfelt relationships with students, and together we form a music ecosystem that is mutually fulfilling. When my students attend my concerts and gigs, my performances inspire and motivate them, and knowing they're in the audience has the same effect on me. I love scheduling informal recitals, performances and social opportunities for them, and being with them as they learn to play a beautiful instrument. Being able to teach what I love is as good for my wellbeing as it is for my pupils' wellbeing, and it serves as a daily reminder that I am on the right path.

MANAGING MONEY

Even though musical performances and teaching provide me with a steady freelance income, I need to manage my money carefully. My income is adequate but modest, so I make sure to live within my means. I also need my finances to have the same order and stability as other aspects of my daily life such as nutrition, movement, and sleep.

Money problems are a leading cause of stress, and for those of us managing a mood disorder or other mental health condition, our finances are an even greater area of concern. It can feel like a low priority, but if a money problem erupts from our lack of attention, it can act as a symptom trigger. Organizing my money and attending to it regularly has made a huge difference in reducing my stress, and has given me peace of mind when other challenges arise in my life.

When I was starting out as a freelancer, my finances were in complete disarray. I still had a consistent part-time job, but I didn't have a system for keeping track of the ebb and flow of my students and gigs, which made it challenging to make long-term plans and goals. I also made frequent impulse purchases without having any sense of what I could spend in any given month, and I didn't know how to budget for my fixed expenses. I could pay my rent, but it was always a crapshoot as to whether I would have the money on time or any left over for other expenses. The unknowns of my finances created a constant, underlying stress. When a friend gushed about meeting with a young, hip financial advisor who set her up with a banking and saving plan tailored to her freelance career, I rushed to make an appointment, and I have been following the plan ever since.

Because I'm self-employed, I need to carefully track my income and expenses for income tax purposes. Math and music are closely related, and you'd think that for someone who loves music so much the math of money and balancing books would be second nature. But it didn't excite me the way that music does, and I found it incredibly tedious. Once I realized it was in my best interest to keep track throughout the year, instead of scrambling at tax time, I established practices and routines to keep things organized. Now I find it ridiculously satisfying and fun to track my earnings and note my expenses, and I love sticking to my budget and watching my savings grow! Managing my money has gone from being a major stressor to a source of confidence and pride, and has given me enormous peace of mind.

I find it easiest to record my income and expenses as I go. There are many simple and user-friendly online tools and apps available that make finances easy and fun to manage. I use these tools nearly every day, often during the breaks I schedule between lessons and gigs. These tools keep my finances organized so that I know exactly what is coming in and what I am spending at all times. They also help me grow my savings and make my finances worry-free so that I can put my energy into the activities I enjoy.

The minimalist philosophy that informs my life helps me safeguard my money and avoid impulsive spending. In addition, I follow two straightforward money practices: I pay myself first (my long-term savings) and I keep an emergency fund in case something happens and I'm unable to work for an extended period.

TAKING CARE OF FUTURE ME: PAYING MYSELF FIRST AND KEEPING AN EMERGENCY FUND

As a self-employed musician who manages a mood disorder, I have developed some practices that keep my finances in order and help me maintain a healthy, organized, stable daily life as free from stress as possible. I often ask myself questions in order to test whether a purchase is necessary, urgent, or wise (these are outlined in Chapter 5). I've also made saving an automatic habit.

Once I established the habit of saving, I didn't realize I was doing it, and the results added up surprisingly quickly. In order to build my savings, I needed to have an idea of how much I was spending each month and what I was spending it on. When I investigated where my money was going each month, I was able to identify unnecessary expenditures that I could direct toward my savings instead. Saving is no longer something I decide to do when I remember, "feel like it," or have extra money; it is a budgeted amount that comes out of my checking account every month, just like my rent and phone bill. It's so encouraging to see the savings and interest add up. When I have a good month or get an unexpected gig, I love stashing away the extra money, knowing I'm taking care of future me.

Being a reliable saver makes me feel accomplished, organized, responsible, and proud. I anticipate paying myself back in the form of a long-awaited vacation or getting a head start on my retirement savings. As a person who earns a modest income with no employer-provided pension, I knew I would have to effectively create my own pension by building a nest egg.

Establishing an emergency fund is another important way that I make sure my future self is taken care of. I prioritized building my emergency fund *first*, before contributing to my savings. I have saved six months' worth of living expenses and keep it liquid in a high-interest savings account. In the event that I find myself unable to work, hospitalized, or without earnings for some unanticipated reason, my emergency fund will cover my fixed expenses in the short term.

My emergency fund is *not* part of my long-term or short-term savings. It is my worst-case-scenario, just-short-of-a-zombie-apocalypse fund. So, when I think of the money that I have, I do not count my emergency fund. It is my baseline. It is *zero* from which I start counting forward. Only after I established an emergency fund did I begin to build long-term and short-term savings for myself. Just knowing that I have this "safety net" gives me peace of mind and a sense of security.

TIPS AND ADVICE FOR SAVING AND MANAGING YOUR MONEY

You may think, as I once did, that you don't make enough money to save or that you have too much debt, but saving has less to do with how much you make and more to do with how much you *spend*. For an informative experiment, try setting aside just $5 a day, the amount you might spend on a fancy coffee beverage (this is known as "The Latte Factor," coined by David Bach). Set up your bank account to automatically move that money so you won't have to think about it. In just two months, you will have saved $300. On the days when you can't seem to complete a single item on your to-do list or even make it out of bed, you will have saved a little for your future. And not having to think about saving means one less thing on your mind.

One of my favorite savings tools is the automatic savings plan within my online banking setup, and I consider my automatic monthly savings to be *part of my fixed expenses*. What's great about an automatic savings function is that you can choose any amount within your means and any time interval you want. I like to save at least 20% of my income monthly, but you can choose a smaller amount on a weekly or even daily basis.

SAVING AN EMERGENCY FUND

An emergency fund is not for improvised spending, and it should not be used to supplement your lifestyle. It is *not* extra cash. If impulse spending is a problem for you, as it has been for me, or if you think you will be tempted to spend your emergency fund, make it less accessible by disabling its connection to your debit card. Consider taking things a step further by keeping your emergency fund at another bank, entirely separate from the financial institution where you maintain your checking account, have a credit card, and pay your bills. Building and preserving an emergency fund is one of many ways that you can care for yourself. Once you have established your fund, thank yourself for taking care of the future you.

CURBING YOUR SPENDING

Cutting back on spending is essential for growing your savings. Before buying something, I always ask myself a few questions. Can I make or borrow this? Is this better than or different from what I already have? What is the cost-per-use? Am I upgrading something, and if so, when am I going to sell / throw out / donate my other item? I like to think: one in, one out! (More in Chapter 5.)

Often there are ways to get what you need without money exchanging hands. Try looking for the item in a local online classified listing such as Kijiji or Craigslist. Consider whether you can source the item another way. Need a special tool? Ask a friend; as a collateral benefit, you'll have the opportunity to catch up with them!

Want to buy a book, movie, or music? Visit your library first. Most libraries have online tools that allow you to put items on hold and have them delivered to a specific branch close to you when they become available. You can also borrow items electronically. This includes ebooks, emagazines, and the use of streaming services for movies and music.

I take small purchases seriously. They often go unnoticed, yet tend to add up quickly. Some examples include drinks and snacks while on the go. I try to minimize these purchases by making my coffee or tea at home, and keeping a water bottle and a bag of raw almonds in my purse. Buying meals is another expense that can add up. I prepare and eat my meals at home when I can, and take homemade food with me if I need to be out during a mealtime. In addition to saving money, this is also healthier. Preserve restaurant visits for special occasions and rare treats.

Need to buy a small gift for someone? If you've been given a gift card as a present and you can't think of anything you absolutely need, consider saving it for the next time you want to buy a gift for someone else. You don't have to spend a cent of your own money this way to show someone you care. Keep your hard-earned savings intact.

And don't forget that you are being marketed to. Ask yourself, am I buying this just because it seems like a great deal? Do I really need this to improve my life? Think about landfills and our planet: where will this item live in 50 years?

CHAPTER 9

People, Places,
and Peaceful Spaces

When you have a mental illness, navigating social situations and managing relationships with others can be challenging, even stressful. My psychotherapist and support group have helped me a great deal, but they cannot shadow me or monitor all of my interactions. In daily life I'm on my own, and have to find ways to take their support with me. I trust and follow the work that I have done, and I remember how important and integral friendships and good relationships are within my family, work life, and community. I think about how these relationships contribute to, support, and enrich my life, but also how I in turn contribute to, support, and enrich the lives of others. I remember that my life, experiences, and recovery matter, but on the whole I am a part of a larger picture: my community, the planet, and the universe.

SOCIALIZING: PORTION CONTROL

I need and want other people in my life. We all do. The issue for those of us managing mood disorders is deciding when and how much of other people to have in our lives. Our relationships need boundaries that work for us.

For me, socializing is like eating. Just as I enjoy coffee breaks, snacks, appetizers *and* full meals, I find that different-sized relationships make for a balanced social life. If I were to eat three full course dinners a day, I would feel weighed down and ill. Likewise, if all of my relationships were as wide and deep as the ones I have with my spouse, best friend, or sibling, my social life would feel too intense. Besides, I need to spread things out. It's impossible for one person to meet all of my needs, and who would want that responsibility anyway?

Friendships are important, and I am always open to meeting people and forming new social relationships. I like meeting and performing with new artists, and I enjoy cordial relations with my cello students. But not all friends have to be best friends. Meal-sized, appetizer-sized, snack or coffee break–sized relationships are all appropriate. The size and intensity varies according to the person and their role: my spouse, doctor, yoga teacher, a good friend from work, a former classmate I meet for lunch a few times a year, or the local barista who remembers my favorite drink order!

Snack-sized relationships are much easier to maintain, and they have fewer expectations. A simple smile for the grocery store cashier, a wave to your mail carrier, or a thank you to the neighbor who shoveled your sidewalk go a long way, and are a good mood booster for both parties. These small interactions contribute to a well-balanced and nourishing social diet. What's more, when I started noticing the "snack-sized" relationships I have (for example, with my yoga teacher, chiropractor, or acquaintances I see occasionally), I realized that spreading out my friendships has relieved those closest to me of the pressure to meet all my social needs.

LIVING GENTLY: PRACTICING EMPATHY WITH YOURSELF AND OTHERS

Managing a mental illness is a 24 / 7 project, a permanent part of your life and who you are. Sometimes, when I feel terrific, I can almost fool myself into thinking that I no longer have an illness or that I no longer need to take medication. I feel "normal." But then I remind myself that elevated moods, like down moods, are temporary. I can embrace and enjoy these moments, but I mustn't assume they are here to stay. Moods are like clouds in the sky: eventually, they pass. This mindful approach comes easily when I feel fine, but when I don't, slogans don't cut it. What I need is gentleness and empathy, from myself and others. Not reassurances that "this too, shall pass," but a recognition of the struggle I am going through and an acknowledgement that, yes, it is a difficult one. In the moment, I try to remind myself that I am doing the best that I can, and that that is enough.

I have a new appreciation for the importance of empathy. Extending empathy to myself was one of the first lessons I learned. When I was diagnosed, I was hung up on labels. I struggled with the idea of being defined as "bipolar." I wondered, *does this mean I'm crazy??* It was hard not to be unkind to myself, and sometimes it still is, especially when I am experiencing a relapse. Over time I let go of the labels and revised how I think of my mental illness. I don't resonate with the statement "I am bipolar." I much prefer to reframe it as "I live *with* bipolar disorder." My illness is something I live *with*, it is not who I am. When I'm experiencing a mood episode, I can say I am depressed or I am manic, because I recognize it as a temporary state, not a defining characteristic. If a person has high blood pressure, they don't say "I am high blood pressure." We are not our health conditions, and I am not mine. Realizing that was an important step in coming to terms with my illness, and being kind to myself even when I am suffering.

When I am unwell it can be nearly impossible to think about anything other than my illness and my needs. But when I am feeling okay, I try to reach out and provide support and empathy to others who are struggling for whatever reason. I make the effort to call a friend who is having a hard time. I attend my support group even if I don't feel I need it, because I might be able to support someone else. Having struggled myself, and been supported by the people in my life, I've come to a better understanding of what real support looks like and how important it is.

At its heart, empathy is the ability to understand, acknowledge, and share the feelings of others, which we demonstrate through communication. This is something I discovered after reading Rosenberg's *Nonviolent Communication* (NVC) on the advice of a yoga teacher / therapist. NVC is based on the premise that everyone has needs, and the practice involves uncovering, acknowledging, and meeting the needs of both parties, and actively practicing empathy through communication, without using blame, shame, guilt, threats, humiliation or coercion. NVC is a communication technique that acknowledges another person's feelings, needs, and requests as a way to make them feel heard, and therefore diffuses anger, defensiveness, and reactivity.

Practicing NVC dramatically changed the way I interact with people in my life. I was astonished to realize that I had been communicating my *entire life* in a way that ignored others' needs—not to mention my own. I would speak quickly and defensively without really hearing or acknowledging the person I was speaking to in any way. I exhibited zero empathy, and my replies used language to "shut down" the conversation, instead of opening up the possibility of true understanding and growth. And I wasn't the only one! Most of the people in my life were doing the same!

Above all, I try to practice empathy actively, by imagining what might be going on for the other person, and what they are *really* experiencing. You can actually practice this by making up scenarios about what the other person might be experiencing. For instance, if a driver cuts you off, you might think, *that driver must be rushing to get to his sick family member before visiting hours are over.* This reframing helps bring awareness and shifts your thoughts away from a knee-jerk reaction (*What a jerk!*) I also love the phrase "be curious, not furious." Asking questions and giving people the benefit of the doubt diffuses blame.

Here are some examples of phrases I use to practice empathy and self-empathy in my day-to-day life:

- Are you feeling rushed? You must need a moment to catch your breath!
- I can't believe I talked non-stop at that party! I was probably feeling really excited.
- I can't imagine what that must have been like for you.
- I imagine that must have been really exciting!
- I'm hearing that there is a lot going on in your life right now.
- I'm sorry I was late. You must have been worried and frustrated!
- I just had a full morning. I am feeling overwhelmed, and I think I need a break.
- It sounds as though you really had a full weekend!
- I'm wondering if a 7:00 pm meeting time feels a little rushed for you.
- That person must be having a really rough day.
- The cashier must be forgetful because she's nearing the end of her shift.
- This project makes me feel confused. I need clarification.

Practicing NVC has resulted in far fewer spats, arguments, "feathers ruffled," or heated misunderstandings with my spouse, family, friends, and students, which has contributed greatly to my mental wellness and the wellbeing of all of the people in my life. Furthermore, practicing empathy-based communication has had a ripple effect that has also been transformative for others in my life.

Here are some simple introductory steps for getting started with nonviolent communication[33]:

1. **State your observation without evaluation.** "I'm noticing that we are out of coffee," states an observed fact, without judgement, while "How could you forget the *coffee*?!" adds an evaluation, which leads to defensiveness.

2. **Identify the feeling that you or the other is experiencing.**
"The idea of not having coffee tomorrow morning makes me feel nervous and worried."

3. **State the need behind that feeling, or identify / guess the others' need and ask.** "I need to start my mornings with a cup of coffee, and running out the night before makes me feel anxious and stressed."

4. **Suggest or request an action to meet the need that was identified.** For the request to be a true request and not a demand, the other person needs to be allowed to decline or propose an alternative. "Drinking coffee in the morning is something I really look forward to and helps me get going. Would you be willing to pick some lattes up for us first thing tomorrow?"

These examples just scratch the surface, but they outline the process of examining how you communicate with your loved ones and community, and the effect that objective statements, non-judgement, practicing empathy and recognizing the needs of others and yourself, and taking actionable steps to have those needs met, can have on your relationships and peace of mind.

EVERYONE ELSE IS WORRIED ABOUT THEM

Another way to promote peace of mind is to remember that everyone is the star of their own movie. When I wasn't feeling wild and unrestrained in my manic episodes, I was sometimes preoccupied with feeling self-conscious and wondering what other people thought of me. It helps to remind myself that people aren't thinking about me nearly as much as I think they are. When I imagine that someone is looking at me as if I'm an idiot, or having thoughts about me in any way, it's because I am feeling insecure and imposing my feelings on them. *Face it*, I tell myself, *most people are preoccupied with their own issues*. They aren't that interested in mine. Living in a bigger city helps with this. To center myself and keep things in perspective, I often switch things around. For example, when I'm tempted to believe that someone else must have a better life / job / family than I do, I reverse it, and conjure up a picture of them comparing themselves to *me*. Then I realize how silly the whole thing is. How could anyone have a realistic sense of my true joys and sorrows from such a distance? And why undermine my relationships with other people by imagining what they may or may not be thinking about me?

TRAVELING WELL

Before my diagnosis, I gave little thought to my comfort while traveling. I spent two years taking a weekly five-hour red-eye bus to work, which seemed just fine on paper, even a little badass. So was cramming several bandmates into one hotel room, or getting into a car full of bassoon players after a concert and driving all night through a snowstorm. I prided myself on being extremely flexible.

I still am flexible in spirit, but as I've already touched on, living with bipolar disorder has meant monitoring every aspect of my day-to-day living: maintaining routine in my sleep and wake cycles, timing my medications, eating right and on time, reducing stress, and understanding and controlling my triggers.

I feel safe and comfortable in my home surroundings and have become so attached to my daily routine that the idea of change comes with a lot of worry, even when traveling to a familiar place like my parents' house. Now, the prospect of travel makes me cautious. I have to protect my wellness. My worries go beyond the usual ones like forgetting to pack something, not being able to adjust to time zone changes, or missing a connection. It's also easy to be afraid of:

- Losing the comfort and reliability of my daily routine
- Not having healthy or familiar food choices
- Getting overwhelmed by my itinerary or being in a new place
- Having my sleep schedule disrupted
- Forgetting to bring or take my medications (or running out)

- Being away from my support system, including my friends, family, doctor, and therapist
- Feeling pressure to "follow the crowd," by getting up early, staying up late, or consuming alcohol (especially challenging when traveling with rock bands)
- Any of the above triggering a manic episode while I am away from home

Before traveling to Asia for work I spoke with my psychiatrist, who told me that the 12-hour time change is so severe for a person with bipolar disorder that the trip alone could cause me to become unstable and trigger a major episode. She told me a story of another patient like me who went to Thailand for a wedding and was irritable and completely destabilized the entire time and ended up not having a good trip at all. I had planned on opting to stay an additional week to sightsee, but with this new information, I compromised by shortening my stay to only two extra days. The idea was that I wouldn't be there long enough to completely shift over to the new time zone, and therefore returning wouldn't be as difficult. My psychiatrist sent me armed with extra medication in the event of an emergency. Making this compromise ensured that everything went smoothly and I had a great time.

For those who also have an anxiety disorder, the stress related to traveling can be magnified. In the days leading up to a trip, I get pretty anxious about all of the unknowns and try to reduce that stress by ensuring that the main details are in place: what time I'm waking up, where I am going, who is driving, where I am staying, and roughly what the itinerary looks like. To get to this stage, I put a lot of time and effort into preparation.

As soon as I figure out my travel dates, I work out as many details as possible. I book off work. I start a packing checklist that I can add to as items occur to me (I like Google Keep). I book my connecting planes, trains, and automobiles, or I confirm them if someone else is doing the booking. I copy the scheduled timing into my calendar. I clarify when I need to meet my transportation and add extra time if there's a border crossing. I determine what time I will need to get up. I triple check that my passport has not expired, and I put it in my bag days ahead to avoid forgetting this biggie. The clearer a picture I can make for myself at this early stage, the better.

Packing early and packing light are key. I start a few days ahead after looking up the weather forecast for my destination, and I go light so I'm not bogged down with too much stuff. Wearing layers while traveling helps keep my bag lighter. Quick-dry items are also great. If need be, I can launder them in a hotel sink and hang them to dry overnight. And I know I can get away with the same pair of pants for more than one day!

It saves me a lot of headaches while I'm away if I remember to pack essentials: the charger for my phone and other items, extra batteries, a water bottle, my eye mask for sleeping, plus tissues, pens, toothbrush and toothpaste. I also consider my aromatherapy rollers and travel pack of herbal teas essential, as they keep me comforted and grounded while traveling. Sometimes I bring along my journal to capture the details of my trip or serve as an outlet on a difficult day.

Most important: I count out my medication and pack a few extra doses. I know my prescription by heart, but I still take a copy of it with me. Also, in case I forget or mix up the time, I set alarms on my phone to remind me when to take my medication. I also make an emergency plan that lists my medications plus warning signs and instructions in the event that I become unwell. The plan has my travel dates along with contact information for important people, such as my doctor, psychiatrist, and therapist. The plan is left with trusted people, and I keep a digital copy, too.

I attend to money matters: visit the bank, get some foreign currency, and call my credit card company to tell them when I'll be traveling so charges while I'm away don't seem suspicious. I purchase travel insurance because I don't want to face thousands of dollars in medical bills in the event that I become hurt or unwell. I also take pictures of the front and back of my credit cards, ID, and bank cards. I email them to myself and print a copy to stash in my bag in case my wallet is lost or stolen. For the trip, my wallet gets purged of nonessentials such as my library card, cheque book, points cards, or unused gift cards.

Above all, I treat myself gently. On the day of my departure, I give myself extra time and don't try to fit in other activities. Inevitably, I remember a few things at the last-minute, and I've learned to give myself breathing room so I don't have to rush, just like my work schedule. If it turns out that I have extra time, I can always visit the restroom, get a snack, read a book, or just breathe. While I'm away, I plan time each day just for relaxing, and, if at all possible, I book myself a recovery day when I return home. I've learned from experience not to hit the ground running as soon as I get back.

In the end, I remind myself that travel is temporary, a privilege, and a luxury, even when it's for work. I'll be home before I know it and will have enjoyed new sights and adventures.

*

I knew that music was my true language at just three years old—a revelation that shaped my entire life. Since then I have traveled the world, I have played with wonderfully accomplished artists in many genres, and I have made a living teaching people the beauty and power of the language of music. These experiences have shown me firsthand the magnitude to which music transcends boundaries and achieves a universality that connects and binds us all. The day I was diagnosed with bipolar disorder, I struggled with the label and with my preconceptions about mental illness. I had to learn a new language to understand my illness and to make the changes necessary in my life and in my mindset to manage it. I had to change the narrative. It is my hope that one day, mental health conditions like mine will be as universally accepted and widely understood as the language of music. Individuals who encounter mental illness will not, as I did, be forced to learn an entirely new vocabulary to understand its implications. In the same way we are all exposed to music in a myriad of ways as children, I hope we will evolve and appreciate a new universal language of awareness, compassion, self-care, empathy and wellbeing. A universal language of mental wellness for every person, whether you have an illness or not. It is my sincere hope that sharing my experience and what I have learned will contribute to the conversation in this new universal language.

CHAPTER 10

Resources

Here is a list of resources for you to explore further.

BOOKS AND WEBSITES ABOUT BIPOLAR DISORDER

- **bphope.com online community for BPHope Magazine.**
  This online community is a terrific resource for people with
  bipolar disorder, as is BPHope Magazine. **bphope.ca**
- **The Bipolar Disorder Survival Guide by David J. Miklowitz.**
  This is a highly recommended, up-to-date, straightforward
  manual for treating and living with bipolar disorder.
- **Loving Someone with Bipolar Disorder by Julie A. Fast and
  John D. Preston.** While intended for spouses of those who
  have bipolar disorder, this guide is helpful for any loved one.
- **Marbles: Mania, Depression, Michelangelo, and Me by Ellen
  Forney.** This wonderfully illustrated graphic novel is a
  beautiful story of a young woman's diagnosis and treatment
  of bipolar disorder.
- **An Unquiet Mind by Kay Redfield Jamison.** This moving
  memoir was one of the first of its kind, written by a
  psychiatrist specializing in mood disorders who has bipolar
  disorder herself.

MENTAL HEALTH ASSOCIATIONS
IN CANADA AND MEETUP GROUPS

- **The Al and Malka Green Artist's Health Centre**. The Artist's Health Centre offers specialized and subsidized care for artists of all disciplines. I have used their services for psychotherapy and various workshops such as one on the artist's concept of self-worth, and performance anxiety. **artistshealth.com**

- **The Canadian Mental Health Association (CMHA)**. CMHA is one of the oldest voluntary services in Canada, providing services and support to over 1.3 million Canadians a year. **cmha.ca**

- **Centre for Addiction and Mental Health (CAMH)**. CAMH is Canada's largest mental health education center, and provides a wide range of services and resources for individuals of all ages and their families. CAMH is where I obtained a second opinion on my diagnosis. **camh.ca**

- **The Mood Disorders Association of Ontario (MDAO)**. MDAO has free weekly drop-in peer support groups with experienced facilitators at multiple locations in Toronto, as well as other services. **mooddisorders.ca**

- **Meetup**. Meetup is a website that brings people together in person, and hosts real-life meeting groups in more categories than you could possibly imagine! There is a large number of mental health groups, from general concerns to specific diagnoses. It is also a great place to find groups for other personal interests, like exercise, nature, and hiking groups. I am a member of the Toronto Bipolar Disorder Bi-weekly Meetup Group, and have participated in others. **meetup.com**

GENERALLY AWESOME BOOKS

- *A New Earth* **by Eckhart Tolle**. In *A New Earth* Tolle expands on *The Power of Now*, his manual on living in the present moment, and focuses on identifying, diffusing and letting go of attachment to the ego, and ego-driven thoughts, words, and actions that cause much dysfunction and unhappiness. Eckhart Tolle is a world-class educator, known for his wisdom and clear writing voice. This book is well-paired with *Nonviolent Communication*.

- ***Big Magic: Creative Living Beyond Fear* by Elizabeth Gilbert**. This is a terrific book about connecting with your innate creativity and taking creative risks, no matter what your profession. It helped me realize that my creativity is a part of me, no matter what.

- ***Daring Greatly* by Dr. Brené Brown**. *Daring Greatly* is about strengthening your courage by embracing vulnerability. I first read Dr. Brown's *The Gifts of Imperfection* (below), and was floored by her TED talk on "The Power of Vulnerability."

- **Nonviolent Communication by Marshall Rosenberg**. When practiced, this technique enhances mutual understanding and social intimacy and diffuses misunderstandings. This book, and developing the practice of nonviolent communication (NVC), revolutionized the way I communicate and interact with every person in my life.

- ***The Artist's Way* by Julia Cameron**. An essential book for any artist, about awakening and connecting with your creativity every day. I enjoyed reading this when I was looking for answers about my career as an artist, and I look forward to reading it again and again.

- ***The Gifts of Imperfection: Let Go of Who You Think You're Supposed to Be and Embrace Who You Are* by Dr. Brené Brown**. This book will encourage you to embrace your whole self, and live what Dr. Brown calls "wholeheartedly." It helped me move forward from viewing myself as just a person with a mental illness.

- ***The Power of Now* by Eckhart Tolle**. This book is a powerful read in strengthening one's practice of mindfulness, letting go of the past and ruminating about the future, and noticing and appreciating the present moment, which is all we have at any given time.

- **The Tools: Transform Your Problems into Courage, Confidence and Creativity by Phil Stutz and Barry Michels.** Written by a psychiatrist and a psychotherapist, this book features actionable tools to help overcome challenges in everyday situations. I read this book to seek help with self-confidence and performance anxiety.
- **Tools of Titans: The Tactics, Routines, and Habits of Billionaires, Icons, and World-Class Performers by Timothy Ferriss.** The title speaks for itself: this is a fantastic collection of lifestyle habits from top performers, including celebrities and athletes, sourced from interviews on the popular podcast *The Tim Ferriss Show*. There are life tools in here for everyone.
- **Tribe of Mentors: Short Life Advice from the Best in the World by Timothy Ferriss.** Described as "the ultimate choose-your-own-adventure book," *Tribe of Mentors* is the ultimate life advice reference book sourced from world-class performers in almost every field. I found dozens of inspiring quotes to live by, and advice and lifestyle practices to follow.
- **You Are Not Your Depression: Finding Light in a Dark Place by Karin Porter.** This is a wonderful little handbook. It is written in a clear voice and is easily comprehended. The author empathizes beautifully with the reader.
- **When the Body Says No: The Cost of Hidden Stress by Dr. Gabor Maté.** You will never think about stress and emotional trauma the same way again. This was recommended to me personally when I was getting ill from chronic stress. Reading it was an enormous "aha!" moment, and it resonated completely.

INSPIRING TED TALKS

- **Got a Meeting? Take a Walk** by Nilofer Merchant
- **How our Microbes Make us Who We Are** by Rob Knight
- **How Sugar Affects the Brain** by Nicole Avena

- ***Tackling the Mental Health Crisis in Our Youth*** by Santa Ono
- ***The Power of Vulnerability*** by Dr. Brené Brown
- ***The Surprisingly Charming Science of Your Gut*** by Giulia Enders
- ***There's No Shame in Taking Care of Your Mental Health*** by Sangu Delle
- ***What's So Funny About Mental Illness?*** by Ruby Wax

FAVORITE BLOGS, WEBSITES AND PODCASTS

- ***A Bipolar, a Schizophrenic, and a Podcast***. Hosted by PsychCentral, bipolar writer and speaker Gabe Howard teams up with Michelle Hammer to present a podcast *by* people with mental illness, *for* people with mental illness. It looks at life through the unique lens of people with depression, bipolar disorder, and schizophrenia. **psychcentral.com/blog/bsp/**

- ***Eckhart Yoga: Yoga Online*** with Esther Eckhart. Different from Eckhart Tolle, Eckhart Yoga is an online yoga studio with fantastic instructors. There are hundreds of different top-notch classes available, of any style and duration of yoga video you could imagine. The annual subscription is great value, and you can easily practice in the comfort of your own home, even for as little as 10 minutes. **eckhartyoga.com**

- ***The Mindful Kind Podcast*** with Rachael Kable. This is a lovely mindfulness podcast with short episodes, a soothing tone, and great tips. Rachael Kable shares some great relatable experiences and insights into her mindfulness journey, and has inspired me to go deeper in mine. rachaelkable.com/podcast

- ***Sound Mind: Living Well with Bipolar: Thriving Ideas For Everyone, Written by a Musician*** by Erika Nielsen. Blog articles have also been featured on **bphope.com**, and the article "Colds and Mental Health Conditions Have More in Common Than You Think!" was voted as "Best of bphope."

- **_Zen Habits: Breathe_** by Leo Baubauta. Even the blog itself is serene and uncluttered, with zero ads. A joy to read. Zen Habits cemented my philosophies of minimalism, non-buying and non-consumerism, slowing down, mindfulness, beginning meditation, finding work-life balance, and combating "busyness." I shared many _Zen Habits_ emails with friends and family, long before social media took off. **zenhabits.net**

REFERENCES

1. **National Institute of Mental Health, Canada**. (2017). Mental Illness. Retrieved from www.nimh.nih.gov/health/statistics/mental-illness.shtml. [accessed 17.10.18]
    Smetanin et al. (2011–2014). The life and economic impact of major mental illnesses in Canada: 2011–2014. Prepared for the Mental Health Commission of Canada. Toronto: RiskAnalytica.

2. **Walker, M**. (2012). Why I tossed out my law degree. Canada: *The Globe and Mail*. Retrieved from www.theglobeandmail.com/life/facts-and-arguments/why-i-tossed-out-my-law-degree/article5233264/ [accessed 04.07.18]

3. **Machado, A**. (1912). 'Proverbios y cantares'. Retrieved from https://en.wikipedia.org/wiki/Antonio_Machado#Works [accessed 18.07.18]

4. **The Centre for Addiction and Mental Health (CAMH)**. (2018). Bipolar Disorder. Retrieved from www.camh.ca/en/health-info/mental-illness-and-addiction-index/bipolar-disorder [accessed 11.10.18]

5. **The Centre for Addiction and Mental Health (CAMH)**. (2018). Bipolar Disorder. Retrieved from www.camh.ca/en/health-info/mental-illness-and-addiction-index/bipolar-disorder [accessed 11.10.18]

6. **The Centre for Addiction and Mental Health (CAMH).** (2018). Bipolar Disorder. Retrieved from www.camh.ca/en/health-info/mental-illness-and-addiction-index/bipolar-disorder [accessed 11.10.18]

7. **The Centre for Addiction and Mental Health (CAMH).** (2018). Bipolar Disorder. Retrieved from www.camh.ca/en/health-info/mental-illness-and-addiction-index/bipolar-disorder [accessed 11.10.18]

8. **The Centre for Addiction and Mental Health (CAMH).** (2018). Bipolar Disorder. Retrieved from www.camh.ca/en/health-info/mental-illness-and-addiction-index/bipolar-disorder [accessed 11.10.18]

9. **American Psychiatric Association**. (2013). *Diagnostic and Statistical Manual of Mental Disorders, Fifth Edition* (DSM-5). Washington, D.C.: American Psychiatric Association Publishing.

10. **Rosenberg, M.B**. (2015). *Nonviolent Communication: A Language of Life*, 3rd Edition. California: PuddleDancer Press.

11. **Maté, G., Ph.D.** (2014). When the Body Says No: Mind/Body Unity and the Stress-Disease Connection [Online video]. Available at: www.youtube.com/watch?v=qlHIWXWDuF0 [accessed 03.10.18]

12. **Deans, E**. (2014). The gut-brain connection, mental illness, and disease. Retrieved from www.sott.net/article/328634-The-gut-brain-connection-mental-illness-and-disease [accessed 15.09.18]

13. **Tuck**. (2018). Stages of Sleep and Sleep Cycles. Retrieved from www.tuck.com/stages/. [accessed 02.05.18]

14. **Lawlis, F. Ph.D**. (2008). The "Mental Breakdown" and the "Sleep" Cure. Retrieved from www.psychologytoday.com/us/blog/redefining-stress/200808/the-mental-breakdown-and-the-sleep-cure. [accessed 02.05.18]

15. **Merchant, N**. (2017). Sitting is the smoking of our generation. Retrieved from www.livemint.com/Science

vCcHBn9LDRDtgEScSEXmUM/Sitting-is-the-smoking-of-our-generation.html. [accessed 03.05.18]

16. **Merchant, N**. (2013). Got a Meeting? Take a Walk. [Online video.] Available at: www.ted.com/talks/nilofer_merchant_got_a_meeting_take_a_walk#t-23751. [accessed 03.05.18]

17. **Preston, J.D. and Fast, J**. (2012) *Loving Someone with Bipolar Disorder: Understanding and Helping Your Partner*. 79. California: New Harbinger Publications.

18. **Preston, J.D. and Fast, J**. (2012) *Loving Someone with Bipolar Disorder: Understanding and Helping Your Partner*. 81–92. California: New Harbinger Publications.

19. **Deans, E**. (2014). The gut-brain connection, mental illness, and disease. Retrieved from www.sott.net/article/328634-The-gut-brain-connection-mental-illness-and-disease [accessed 15.09.18]

20. **Carabotti, M., Scirocco, A., Maselli, M. A., & Severi, C**. (2015). The gut-brain axis: interactions between enteric microbiota, central and enteric nervous systems. *Annals of Gastroenterology: Quarterly Publication of the Hellenic Society of Gastroenterology*, 28(2), 203–9.

21. **Dickerson, F., Severance, E., Yolken, R**., (2017). The microbiome, immunity, and schizophrenia and bipolar disorder. *Brain, Behavior, and Immunity*, 62, 46–52.

22. **Köhler, O., Krogh, J., Mors, O., & Benros, M. E**. (2016). Inflammation in Depression and the Potential for Anti-Inflammatory Treatment. *Current Neuropharmacology*, 14(7), 732–42.

23. **Muneer, A**. (2016). Bipolar Disorder: Role of Inflammation and the Development of Disease Biomarkers. *Psychiatry Investigation*, 13(1), 18–33.

24. **Alnuweiri, Tamim**. (2018). An inflammatory diet could impact your mental health, new research shows. Retrieved from www.wellandgood.com/good-advice/inflammation-mental-health-connection-study/. [accessed 14.06.18]

Medaris Miller, A. (2018). Can an Anti-Inflammatory Diet Improve Your Mental Health? Retrieved from https://health.usnews.com/wellness/articles/2018-08-27/can-an-anti-inflammatory-diet-improve-your-mental-health [accessed 03.09.18]

Integrative Psychiatry. (2012). Brain Inflammation. Retrieved from www.integrativepsychiatry.net/brain_inflammation.html [accessed 03.09.18]

Cairn, J. (2018). Anti-Inflammatory Foods: The Complete Guide to Treating Inflammation Through Diet. Retrieved from www.thegoodgut.org/guide-to-anti-inflammatory-foods/. [accessed 06.09.18]

25. **Carey-Simos, G**. (2015). How Much Data Is Generated Every Minute On Social Media? Retrieved from http://wersm.com/how-much-data-is-generated-every-minute-on-social-media/. [accessed 11.03.17]

26. **SWNS**. (2017). Americans check their phones 80 times a day: study. Retrieved from https://nypost.com/2017/11/08/americans-check-their-phones-80-times-a-day-study/. [accessed 11.03.17]

27. **Dunckley, V.L., M.D**. (2012). Electronic Screen Syndrome: An Unrecognized Disorder? Retrieved from www.psychologytoday.com/ca/blog/mental-wealth/201207/electronic-screen-syndrome-unrecognized-disorder. [accessed 13.03.17]

28. **Harvard Medical School**. (2015). Having a dog can help your heart – literally. Retrieved from www.health.harvard.edu/staying-healthy/having-a-dog-can-help-your-heart-literally. [accessed 13.03.17]

29. **Porter, K**. (2018). *You Are Not Your Depression: Finding Light in a Dark Place*. Victoria, BC: FriesenPress.

30. **Psychological projection**. (Last revision date 17 October 2018). In *Wikipedia*. Retrieved from https://en.wikipedia.org/wiki/Psychological_projection. [accessed 18.10.18]

31. **Sanicas, M**. (2017) Depression & Vitamin D Deficiency: Is There A Connection? Retrieved from https://medium.com/@melvin.sanicas/depression-vitamin-d-deficiency-is-there-a-connection-1d2fefb45da2. [accessed 11.15.18]

Jankovic, J., McDonald, L., & Johnston-Webber, C. (2012). Vitamin D and the perinatal period in women suffering from schizophrenia. *Mental Health in Family Medicine*, 9(4), 215–17.

Vieth, R., Kimball, S., Hu, A., & Walfish, P. G. (2004). Randomized comparison of the effects of the vitamin D_3 adequate intake versus 100 mcg (4000 IU) per day on biochemical responses and the wellbeing of patients. *Nutrition Journal*, 3, 8.

Jorde, R., Sneve, M., Figenschau, Y., Svartberg, J., Waterloo, K. (2008). Effects of vitamin D supplementation on symptoms of depression in overweight and obese subjects: randomized double blind trial. *Journal of Internal Medicine*, 264(6), 599–609.

McGrath, J., Saari, K., Hakko, H., Jokelainen, J., Jones, P., Järvelin, MR., Chant, D., Isohanni, M. (2004). Vitamin D supplementation during the first year of life and risk of schizophrenia: a Finnish birth cohort study. *Schizophrenia Research*, 67 (2–3): 237–45.

32. **Greenblatt, J**. M. (2011). Psychological Consequences of Vitamin D Deficiency. Retrieved from www.psychologytoday.com/ca/blog/the-breakthrough-depression-solution/201111/psychological-consequences-vitamin-d-deficiency. [accessed 10.10.18]

33. **Wikihow**. (n.d) How to Practice Nonviolent Communication. Retrieved from www.wikihow.com/Practice-Nonviolent-Communication. [accessed 13.05.17]

ACKNOWLEDGEMENTS

Let chaos storm!
Let cloud shapes swarm!
I wait for form.

Robert Frost

I extend my heartfelt thanks to these extraordinary people who made *Sound Mind* possible.

Anne Stilman, for putting me in touch with your wonderful husband, Greg Ioannou, publishing guru. Greg, you guided me from query to manuscript and helped me believe that this message was important. This book is thanks to you, and the people you connected me to who helped shape it along the way.

Genevieve Chornenki, you formed this book from the inside-out. I am incredibly grateful for your wordsmithing, and your friendship. Kathryn Willms, I could not have crossed the finish line without you. Kelvin Kong, I am honoured to be on your list at K2 Literary. Thanks also to Sam Hiyate, Jaye Marsh, Kate Unrau, and Jaclyn Law.

To my fantastic team at Trigger Publishing, I am delighted that *Sound Mind* found a home with you. Special thanks to Hannah Abrahaley and the design team, and to my brilliant editor, Stephanie Cox.

My deepest gratitude to Jackie Jenkins, Dr. Sivan Bega, Dr. Sagar Parikh, Dr. Gaiathry Jeyarajan, and Dr. Kate Greenaway.

To Ellen Forney, Julie A. Fast, and Kay Redfield Jamison, for your inspiration. To Liz Parker, for your expert styling and advice, and to Shayne Gray, for your stunning photography. To the community at bphope.com, I look forward to keeping the conversation going.

To my loving family and friends near and far, thank you for being so graciously amenable to being in this book, and for supporting me in sharing this story. Special thanks to Elizabeth Lance, Livia Simas, and Amanda Ricci. Thanks also to Caitlin Wellman, Weronika Zielinska, Tim Marskell, and Ryan Gillespie.

To the music community of Kingston, Ontario, for being my first home in music, especially Queen's University. To Wolf Tormann, for your wonderful years of mentorship, and to David Hetherington at the Glenn Gould School. To friends and colleagues at the Sudbury Symphony Orchestra, our years together are forever in my heart.

Finally, most especially, thank you to my other half, Graham Smith. For your honest feedback and tireless council. For your astute eye and tag-team editing sessions. For all the amazing meals, favorite snacks, and bottomless cups of tea. For being the shoulder I lean on and the boulder of unconditional love and support that makes everything else possible. Thank you for being my partner, through chaos and composure. I love you.

**If you found this book interesting ...
why not read these next?**

Teacup In A Storm

Finding My Psychiatrist

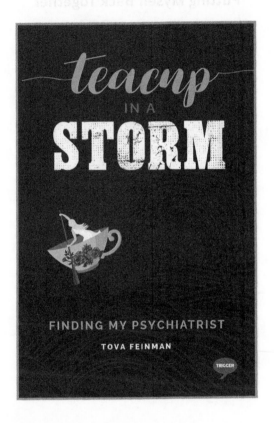

Wracked with trauma from childhood abuse, Tova sought therapy to soothe her mind. However, it is not as easy as simply finding a person to talk to ...

Sex, Suicide & Serotonin

Taking Myself Apart,
Putting Myself Back Together

When Debbie Hampton took the mix of wine and drugs that nearly killed her, she didn't ever want to wake up – but she did, and her problems were only just beginning. In this book, Debbie tells the inspirational story of how she forged a new life for herself.

Walk A Mile Book

Tales of a Wandering Loon

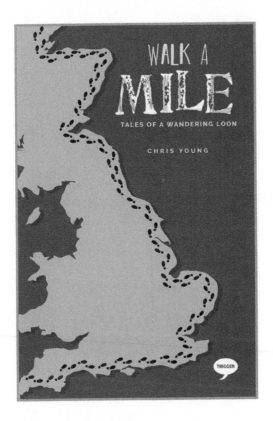

Chris Young was all too aware of the stigma surrounding BPD. And so he decided to walk around the edge of the UK – as many with mental illness feel they belong on the edge of society – and challenge mental health stigma, one conversation at a time.

the *Shaw* mind
FOUNDATION

Creating hope for children,
adults and families

Sign up to our charity, The Shaw Mind Foundation
www.shawmindfoundation.org
and keep in touch with us; we would love to hear
from you.

*We aim to bring to an end the suffering and despair caused
by mental health issues. Our goal is to make help and support
available for every single person in society, from all walks of
life. We will never stop offering hope. These are our promises.*

TRIGGER™
The voice of mental health

www.triggerpublishing.com

Trigger is a publishing house devoted to opening conversations about mental health. We tell the stories of people who have suffered from mental illnesses and recovered, so that others may learn from them.

Adam Shaw is a worldwide mental health advocate and philanthropist. Now in recovery from mental health issues, he is committed to helping others suffering from debilitating mental health issues through the global charity he co-founded, The Shaw Mind Foundation. www.shawmindfoundation.org

Lauren Callaghan (CPsychol, PGDipClinPsych, PgCert, MA (hons), LLB (hons), BA), born and educated in New Zealand, is an innovative industry-leading psychologist based in London, United Kingdom. Lauren has worked with children and young people, and their families, in a number of clinical settings providing evidence based treatments for a range of illnesses, including anxiety and obsessional problems. She was a psychologist at the specialist national treatment centres for severe obsessional problems in the UK and is renowned as an expert in the field of mental health, recognised for diagnosing and successfully treating OCD and anxiety related illnesses in particular. In addition to appearing as a treating clinician in the critically acclaimed and BAFTA award-winning documentary *Bedlam*, Lauren is a frequent guest speaker on mental health conditions in the media and at academic conferences. Lauren also acts as a guest lecturer and honorary researcher at the Institute of Psychiatry Kings College, UCL.

Please visit the link below:

www.triggerpublishing.com

Join us and follow us...

@triggerpub

Search for us on Facebook